D1206336

THE THEORIES OF CLAUDE DEBUSSY

Musicien français

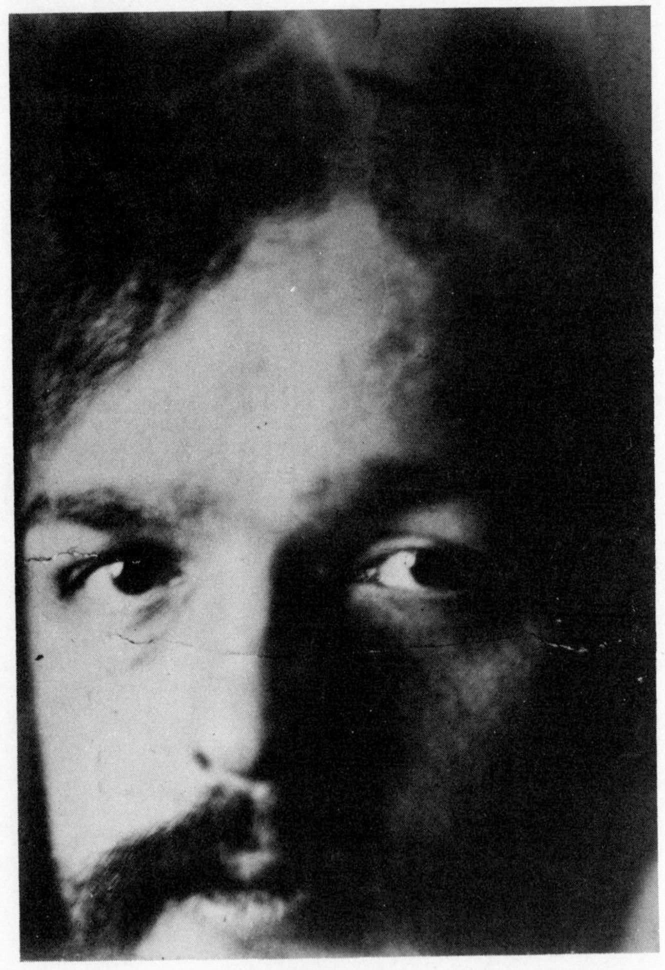

CLAUDE DEBUSSY

From a photograph by Pierre Louÿs

THE THEORIES OF CLAUDE DEBUSSY

Musicien français

LÉON VALLAS

Translated from the French by
MAIRE O'BRIEN

DOVER PUBLICATIONS, INC.
NEW YORK

Published in Canada by General Publishing Company, Ltd., 30 Lesmill Road, Don Mills, Toronto, Ontario.

Published in the United Kingdom by Constable and Company, Ltd., 10 Orange Street, London WC 2.

This Dover edition, first published in 1967, is an unabridged and unaltered republication of the work originally published in 1929 by Oxford University Press, London.

This edition is published by special arrangement with Oxford University Press, Inc. 417 Fifth Avenue, New York, N.Y. 10016.

Library of Congress Catalog Card Number: 67-16703

Manufactured in the United States of America
Dover Publications, Inc.
180 Varick Street
New York, N.Y. 10014

PREFACE

CLAUDE DEBUSSY was no lover of publicity. He tells us himself that he never worried about what people said of his music. He went his way quietly, without seeking to advertise his theories. Nevertheless, in his riper years he frequently published his opinions on music. Sometimes these appeared from his own pen, in publications of the day; sometimes they were reproduced, more or less accurately, from interviews; for in spite of an instinctive repugnance, he could not always refuse importunate journalists.

It was late in the day when Debussy made his debut as a musical critic. He was close on forty when, in 1901, he became musical critic to the *Revue Blanche*. He had not then made his mark as the composer of 'Pelléas et Mélisande'; and though he had already attracted the attention of musicians by such works as the 'Prélude à l'après-midi d'un Faune' (1892), the String Quartet (1893), or the Chansons de Bilitis (1898), the general public looked upon him merely as a revolutionary. His compositions were appreciated only by a small group. The mocking tone and the paradoxical views of his critiques only served to increase his reputation as a disturbing if not a dangerous artist. For, as the Sar Péladan puts it, did he not dare to utter blasphemies against acknowledged masterpieces and their creators, and to show contempt for the Holy of Holies?

He contributed eight articles to the *Revue Blanche* in as many months. The publication had, however, but a small circulation, limited to advanced intellectual circles, and his work remained practically unnoticed.

In January 1903, after a year of literary inactivity the beginning of which had been marked by the production of 'Pelléas et Mélisande' at the Opéra-Comique, Debussy was about to become musical critic of the *Renaissance Latine*. M. Calvocoressi had indeed announced this fact officially in an article published on December 15th, 1902. Then came a sudden change in the editorship of this review, and the first contribution which Debussy had sent in (the proof-sheets of which had even been corrected) did not appear.

Meanwhile the musician had promised his co-operation to a Paris daily—*Gil Blas*—and the article that had been destined for the *Renaissance Latine* was the second to appear in that paper.

In the course of six months twenty articles appeared in *Gil Blas*—usually on Mondays—and four short critiques on first performances.

Preface

Debussy, writing to M. Jean-Aubry in 1908, told of hours of tedium, the result of this too regular work which obliged him to write notices of all sorts of music. Occasionally, on days of publication, he simply re-wrote old opinions that had already appeared in the *Revue Blanche*. These articles were widely read, at least in Paris, and were sometimes reproduced or quoted in musical reviews. Their biting irony and mocking tone, and the frequent use of paradox, prevented many earnest musicians from taking them seriously.

In the ten years between July 1903 and November 1912 Claude Debussy refused all journalistic work. During this period he published or allowed to be published only a very few articles or answers to inquiries, and these were frequently disdainful and ironical. It took all the friendly persistence of one of his most fervent disciples—Émile Vuillermoz—to induce him to change his mind. At last the editor of the review 'S.I.M.' obtained Debussy's promise of collaboration for the winter of 1912–13 and subsequent seasons. This enabled him to give each month the opinions of two such authorities as the composers of 'Pelléas' and of 'Fervaal', whose followers set up one against the other as rivals if not as enemies.

In the course of the two seasons preceding the

war, 'S.I.M.' published ten articles by Debussy. These were composed in part of what the author himself admits to be 'notes that were much too hastily written'.

At this time he was somewhat hampered by the role of leader or head of a 'school' which was being thrust upon him in opposition to his friend Vincent d'Indy. Over-zealous partisans involved him in controversy and drove him to accentuate his prejudices and overstate his theories.

Debussy's musical critiques, a complete list of which appears farther on, and his answers to questions on music, the greater number if not all of which we have collected, are scattered in publications that are no longer available. Only a certain number of his articles have been collected in book form, a limited edition of which appeared after the author's death. The invaluable opinions of the great musician are therefore unknown to the general public. Consequently we have thought it advisable to collect them, to arrange them in clear and simple form; and so to place within the reach of all, not the articles themselves, but the theories which they contain, embodying the musical opinions of one of our most original composers.

In his writings there recurs one outstanding precept (which might be emphasized by endless commentary), instructive and of lasting value, based as it is on a sincere love of music and a constant zeal for artistic independence and rejuvenation: a passionate belief in the destiny of French national art.

In spite of their impromptu composition, their humorous tone and the careless looseness of the style, the theories expressed in these articles are not unworthy of the great artist who, with all his originality and freedom, prided himself on his connexion with the time-old tradition of his country. Here we find, fully and definitely stated, the ideas which are delicately hinted at in his music, the meaning of which we sense when we listen to his compositions. Gabriel d'Annunzio, his collaborator, called him 'Claude de France'; and he himself inscribed his last works, written during the war, with the proud, simple signature: Claude Debussy, musicien français.[1]

[1] Articles dealing with Debussy as a musical critic have appeared as follows: by M. D. Calvocoressi (*Renaissance Latine*, Dec. 15th, 1902), Marc Pincherle (*Echo Musical*, Nov. 1919), G. Jean-Aubry (*Revue Musical*, Dec. 1920).

The letter reproduced in facsimile was addressed to M. D. Calvocoressi on the subject of his projected collaboration with *Renaissance Latine*.

The photograph which appears as frontispiece, and which is by Pierre Louÿs, is published for the first time. It was kindly placed at our disposal by Madame Claude Debussy.

Dimanche

28 Déc /02

Cher Monsieur,

permettez-moi de vous dire que je ne me suis dégagé de la Renaissance Latine qu'à la suite d'une entente que je moyennais entière entre les directeurs du Gil Blas et la direction de la Renaissance. Il faut aussi que vous sachiez mon intention de faire un feuilleton sur la musique et non un article aux lendemains des différentes premières. Si j'avais plus de temps votre combinaison aurait pu me plaire, mais il est impossible que j'abandonne toute idée de faire de la musique, d'où le souci de me conserver un peu de loisir.

Je ne demande qu'à être agréable à "la Renaissance" mais vous m'accorderez qu'il me reste bien peu de jours? Ne pourriez-vous pas attendre jusqu'au 2 janvier?

— Il faudra que j'aille à Bruxelles pour la 1re de "l'Etranger" ce qui me prendra encore deux jours, au minimum.

Croyez à mon regret de tout cela et à mon cordial désir de vous satisfaire.

Claude Debussy.

58. rue Cardinet.

CONTENTS

I

Profession of faith and outlook on Criticism. Love of Music. Love of Nature.

IN his first contribution to the *Revue Blanche* Debussy made a clear and brief profession of ardent faith. The new author had suffered too keenly from the unintelligent and unfeeling censure of his colleagues to imitate them. 'Criticism', he says, 'too often resembles brilliant variations on the theme: You went wrong because you did not do as I do, or else: You are talented, I am not. This won't do.' Therefore, Debussy determines to confine himself to 'sincere impressions actually experienced'. He endeavours 'to discover in works the various impulses that gave them birth, and what they contain of inner life'. Here there is none of that immature work to which so many writers on music are condemned for life because of their lack of true feeling; no minute dissection, treating as corpses scores that are full of life. He avoids also the 'game which consists in taking them to pieces, as though they were watches of curious construction. If people would only remember that as children they were forbidden to open the insides of dolls . . . (surely in itself an outrage on mystery). No: they still insist on sticking their aesthetic noses where they have no business. They no longer cut open the doll, perhaps; but they explain it, take it to pieces, and thus kill the mystery in cold blood. It is more convenient; moreover, it gives them something to talk about. Utter ignorance may excuse some, to be sure; but others, more vicious, do the harm with malice aforethought. Mediocrity must be defended at all costs, and those who undertake its defence can always rely on support.'

At the close of his declaration of principles our critic repeats: 'I should like to insist on the use of this term *Impressions*, which I value because it enables me to shield my emotion from any parasitic aesthetics.'

Two years later, when he took over the musical column of *Gil Blas*, Debussy recalled his critical essay published in the *Revue Blanche* which, he wrote, had been 'preceded by certain explanations couched more or less in these terms', and he reproduced the lines given above. In the new version the wording is slightly altered and the following interpolation occurs regarding the deliberate malignity of those fierce critics who love to destroy all mystery: 'It is practically what Thomas de Quincey, the celebrated opium-eater, calls *murder considered as one of the fine arts*.'

He concludes the renewal of his profession of faith as an impressionist with the following lines: 'May the gods and Music forgive me: I have not altered my opinions, and in this feuilleton which *Gil Blas* has done me the honour to entrust to me, I shall endeavour in my criticisms to keep to impressions as far as possible free from arbitrary aesthetics.'

In one of his articles written in 1913 he repeats once more how essential it is for a critic to refrain from destroying the mystery of music. 'Let us maintain that the beauty of a work of art must always remain mysterious; that is to say, that it is impossible to explain exactly how it is created. Let us at all costs preserve this magic peculiar to music, for of all the arts it is the most susceptible to magic.

'When the god Pan put together the seven pipes of the syrinx, he imitated at first only the long melancholy note of the frog voicing its complaint to the moon. Later, he entered into competition with the birds. It is probably since that time that the birds have added to their repertory. Such origins are sacred, and music may well take pride in them and endeavour to preserve their mystery. . . . In the name of all the gods, let us not attempt to destroy or explain it.'

In dealing with questions of art, Debussy has no intention of borrowing the 'classical jargon that lends us fluency' either from the critics, 'very worthy folk who know nothing about music (and can therefore approach the subject with true disinterestedness)', or from his new colleagues, 'journalists and penny-a-liners', of whom Monsieur Croche[1] declared that their opinion was of no importance.

Monsieur Croche, 'an old fool whose love for music takes a form as inexcusable as it is intolerant',

[1] Monsieur Croche, who gave his name to the volume of Debussy's posthumous articles ('Monsieur Croche, antidilettante', now published in English as *Monsieur Croche, Dilettante Hater*—Dover reprint, 1962), is an imaginary personage, 'the ghost of voices now silent'. His two meetings and his conversations with Debussy, provide the composer-critic with a peg on which to hang his own more surprising theories—theories which twenty-five years ago ran the risk of being considered scandalously blasphemous.

looked upon this sonorous art from a peculiar angle and would 'refer to an orchestral score as though it were a picture, rarely using technical terms, but expressing himself in unusual words of a dull, out-of-date elegance that had an old-fashioned ring. The new critic expresses the thoughts inspired by his musical passion in language akin to that of his phantom friend. This passion may appear, to some at least, to be likewise intolerant and inexcusable. But there is nothing narrow about it. It is not limited to *one* brand of music but embraces all music.

Too many musicians, both professionals and amateurs, take pleasure in one form of art alone and remain 'jealously faithful to it despite its wrinkles and its paint'.

Debussy states these opinions without pompous affectation; he does not cling desperately to his own past experiences to set up a standard of comparison and thus condemn the present in the name of the past. 'I try to forget music, because it might hamper me when I hear music that I do not now know, but may know to-morrow. . . . Why cling to what one knows only too well?' He does not aim at the cold serenity, the impassivity of wisdom grown old. He is a man. He is in love. Music is a woman. So his criticism must be a work of passion: 'I love music too much to be able to speak of it otherwise than with passion. Shall I even succeed in avoiding that faint suggestion of bias which colours the best of motives and causes the most convinced advocate to lose his head? I dare not hope it. Those to whom art is a passion are the most uncompromising lovers.

Besides, it is impossible to realize how completely music is feminine, which goes perhaps to explain why chastity is so common in men of genius.'

This love of music, which alone should create the desire to write on artistic productions, is not very general in those who make it their profession to write of them. 'Notice the tone in which critics write. How evident it is that they have no love for music! They seem to cherish some obscure grudge, some old, persistent hatred. And this attitude is not peculiar to our times: in all ages there have been people who regarded beauty as a veiled insult to themselves. They instinctively seek to avenge themselves by degrading the ideal that humiliates them. How far removed is this odious frame of mind from the just severity of such a one as Saint-Beuve, who loved literature, or Baudelaire, who was both a marvellous artist and a critic of unique judgement.'

One passion only—Debussy declares in his first page—can compete with and sometimes out-rival the love of music, and that is the love of nature.

The critic has every intention of attending the Sunday Concerts. However, 'on those Sundays when God is kind', he is quite prepared to neglect a duty essential to his profession—and desert Colonne or Lamoureux for the sake of an outing. . . . Then, only some extraordinary attraction such as a concert by Nikisch will induce him to remain shut up in a hall. 'On Sunday, 19th of May, a burning and relentless sun seemed to mock at all attempt to listen to music of any description. The Berlin Philharmonic Orchestra conducted by Mr. A. Nikisch had fixed on that day for their first concert. I trust that Providence will forgive me for being false to my resolutions, and that others more fortunate than I will have paid to the green sward their customary tribute of sausage-skins and love-making.'

His great love of nature often finds expression in his articles. Sometimes Debussy evokes the ever-new splendour of the world in a veritable canvas of literary colour. 'I had lingered', he says, 'in autumn-filled landscapes, bound by the spell of ancient forests. The golden leaves, as they fell from the agonized trees, and the shrill angelus bell, bidding the fields take their sleep, sent up a sweet, persuasive voice that counselled complete forgetfulness. In solitary state the sun sank to rest. Not a single peasant was there to strike a stereotyped attitude in the foreground. Beasts and men went quietly homewards, their humble task accomplished whose beauty had this advantage, that it invited neither praise nor blame....'

In this pastoral setting the musician is at once at peace. He even succeeds in forgetting the world of music with its futile struggles, its prejudices and its ugliness. These can no longer spoil his pleasure in the real beauty of music. 'How far away were those discussions on art in which the names of great men sometimes sound like swear-words! Forgotten was the petty fever of first-night performances. I was alone and delightfully unconcerned. Never, perhaps, did I love music more than at this period when I never heard it mentioned. I saw it entire in its beauty and not in symphonic fragments or feverish and scrappy lyrics.'

And how sorry he was to leave the country!

'I had to leave this peaceful joy,' he says, 'and return to town, driven by that city superstition which makes so many men willing to be crushed so long as they share in the momentum the mechanism of which they are unconsciously a part.'

This attitude led Debussy to praise composers such as Weber, who profited by the lessons they received direct from nature, and to censure great masters, including Beethoven and Berlioz, whose vision was warped by reading. It likewise prompted him to give, in terms of nature, definitions of art which, in a few phrases full of his own peculiar elegance, summarize what one hardly dares to describe as the aesthetics and pedagogy of Debussy.

II

Definition of Music as a Free Art

'MUSIC is a mysterious form of mathematics whose elements are derived from the infinite. Music is the expression of the movement of the waters, the play of curves described by changing breezes. There is nothing more musical than a sunset. He who feels what he sees will find no more beautiful example of development in all that book which, alas, musicians read but too little—the book of Nature....'

This statement which Debussy wrote in 1903 is the same, though differently expressed, as the one he had previously put into the mouth of Monsieur Croche: 'Music is the sum total of scattered forces.... And people have made of it a song composed of theories! I prefer a few notes from the flute of an Egyptian shepherd. He collaborates with the scenery around him and hears harmonies of which our textbooks are ignorant. . . . Musicians listen only to music written by skilful hands; they never hear what is written in Nature. There is more to be gained by seeing the sun rise than by hearing the Pastoral Symphony.'

The definition becomes a clear-cut precept when Monsieur Croche declares that the artist should 'take counsel of no man, but only of the passing wind that tells us the story of the world'.

The same theory occurs in a more developed form in the monthly 'S.I.M.' of November 1913: 'Our symphonic painters do not devote sufficiently fervent attention to the beauty of the seasons. They study Nature in works which depict her in an unpleasantly artificial aspect, where the rocks are of cardboard and the leaves of painted gauze. Yet, of all the arts, music is closest to nature—offers her the most subtle attraction. Although they claim to be nature's sworn interpreters, painters and sculptors can give us but a loose and fragmentary rendering of the beauty of the universe. Only one aspect, one instant is seized and placed on record. To musicians only is it given to capture all the poetry of night and day, of earth and heaven, to reconstruct their atmosphere and record the rhythm of their great heart-beats. They do not abuse this privilege. Only rarely does nature draw from them one of those sincere outbursts of love which delight us in certain pages of "Freischütz". More often than not, their passion is satisfied with leaves that literature has dried between the pages of its books. With such was Berlioz content all his life. His genius found bitter pleasure in airing its longings in an artificial-flower shop.'

He repeats this theory more personally and definitely, in an answer to an inquiry in *Comœdia*: 'We do not listen to the thousand sounds with which nature surrounds us. We are not sufficiently on the alert to hear this varied music which she so generously offers. It envelops us, and yet we have lived in its midst until now, ignoring it. This, to my mind, is the new path. But believe me, I have but caught a glimpse of it. Much remains to be done and he who does it . . . will be a great man!'

During the year 1911, when Debussy gave interviews to various journalists, he repeats the same idea in different forms.

One day he was asked if it were not a fact that 'Pelléas et Mélisande' would be produced in several foreign towns.

'I can't tell you anything definite,' he replied; 'I know absolutely nothing about it—besides, my interest does not lie there: it is in music, in music that one composes, that one loves! I myself love music passionately; and because I love it, I try to free it from barren traditions that stifle it. It is a free art, gushing forth, an open air art, an art boundless as the elements, the wind, the sky, the sea! It must never be shut in and become an academic art.'

Speaking to an Austrian journalist a few months later, he again stresses his desire for freedom in the interpretation of nature: 'I am all for liberty. Music by its very nature is free. Every sound you hear around you can be reproduced. Everything that a keen ear perceives in the rhythm of the surrounding world can be represented musically. To some people rules are of primary importance. But my desire is to reproduce only what I hear. . . .'

In his opinion, music was not intended 'to reproduce nature more or less exactly, but to receive the mysterious accord that exists between nature and the imagination'.

Debussy dreamed always of the liberation of music by nature, and in *Gil Blas* as in the *Revue Blanche* he developed his theory of growth and rejuvenation through life in the open. He deplored the fact that military bands monopolized the Squares, making among the trees 'the noise of an infant phonograph'. He loved to picture festivals which should be 'more completely in keeping with the natural scenery. Trees called for a numerous orchestra with the co-operation of the human voice. (No, *not* a choral society, thanks!) I can imagine a music specially designed for the open air, all on big lines, with daring instrumental and vocal effects which would have full play in the open and soar joyfully to the tree-tops. Certain harmonic progressions which sound abnormal within the four walls of a concert hall would surely find their true value in the open air. Perhaps this might be a means of doing away with these little affectations of over-precision in form and tonality which so encumber music. Thus art might find regeneration and learn the beautiful lesson of freedom from the efflorescence of the trees. Would it not gain in grandeur anything that it might lose in charm of detail? It should be understood that vastness of effect should be aimed at and not bulk. Neither should one weary the echoes with the repetition of excessive sounds. One should rather make use of them in order to prolong the harmonious dream. So, the very air, the movement of the leaves, and the perfume of flowers would work together in mysterious union with music which would thus bring all the elements into such natural harmony that it would seem to form a part of each.... In this way it could be proved without a doubt that music and poetry, alone of the arts, dwell in space. . . . I may be mistaken, but it is my belief that this idea will be the dream of future generations. In our day music will, I fear, continue to be rather stuffy.'

When Debussy remodelled for *Gil Blas* the article already referred to that had previously appeared in the *Revue Blanche*, he added the following words which further emphasize his thoughts on free, open-air music: 'And the kind, quiet trees would represent the pipes of a universal organ, offering the support of their branches to clusters of children who would learn the charming roundelays of long ago—now, alas, replaced by the inept refrains that dishonour the gardens and towns of to-day. At the same time, we should rediscover that counterpoint of which we have made a task for pedants, but from which the old composers of the French Renaissance could draw a smile.'

This craze for pedantic mannerisms in musical circles, which Debussy never lost an opportunity of condemning, is no more admissible in so-called scholarly music than in folk-music. For art cannot be reduced to the level of a mere intellectual trick. It satisfies a human desire for oblivion and illusion.

'Art is the most beautiful deception: and no matter how much a man may wish to make it the setting for his daily life, he must still desire that it remain an illusion lest it become utilitarian, and as dreary as a workshop. Do not the masses as well as the select few seek therein oblivion, which is in itself a form of deception? The smile of Mona Lisa probably never really existed,—still its charm is eternal. Let us then avoid disillusioning any one by clothing the dream with too much reality. Let us be satisfied with interpretations that are the more consoling because of their undying beauty.'

The artist's aim 'is similar to that of Solness, the Master Builder (one of the last of Ibsen's dramas), which is to construct for the children of men a house wherein they will be happy and at home. . . .'

On one occasion Debussy did not hesitate to express his theory in a statement which made a sensation,—for those were the days when musical intellectualism was at its height. In praising Massenet for having understood the true role of a composer—one who does not base his art on calculations—he declared: 'Music should humbly seek to please; within these limits great beauty may perhaps be found. Extreme complication is contrary to art. Beauty must appeal to the senses, must provide us with immediate enjoyment, must impress us or insinuate itself into us without any effort on our part. Take Leonardo da Vinci; take Mozart: these are the great artists!'

Couperin and Rameau must also be classed among the great artists for this very reason, that being French musicians they have, following the national tradition, wished 'above all to give pleasure'.

Let us discover what we can of Debussy's innermost mind from these opinions, extravagantly worded and distorted though they be by the very natural prejudice existing at the beginning of the century against the intellectual excesses of the followers of d'Indy. As he says himself, he preferred 'music as Mussorgsky felt it' to music 'as Dukas and some others understood it'.

About the year 1905 it needed a good deal of civic courage to make such a strong stand against the pedantic forms then in vogue in symphonic art. The French musician protested instinctively, but none the less deliberately, for in these affectations he discerned a form of corruption of Germanic origin, which was fraught with dire consequences for France.

One day, in the course of an interview (for which he had been asked), Debussy, trembling at his own audacity, declared that 'music until the present day has rested on a false principle. There is too much *writing* of music. Music is made for its effect on paper although it is intended for the ear. Too much importance is attached to the writing of music, the formula, the craft. Composers seek their ideas within themselves when they should look around for them. They combine, construct, imagine themes in which to express ideas. These are developed; they are modified when they encounter other themes representing other ideas. All this is metaphysics, it is not music. The latter should be spontaneously registered by the ear of the listener without his having to discover abstract ideas in the meanderings of a complicated development.'

When he was writing the score of the 'Martyre de Saint Sébastien', he delighted in extolling the freedom of music, an open-air art, and in denouncing academic excesses.

'Composition as a craft', he says, 'is no doubt very

fine. I used to be enthusiastic about it myself. But I have given much time to reflection, and the writing itself might with advantage be simplified, the means of expression made more direct....'

His study of pure music had led him, as he tells us in a statement concerning 'Pelléas' which is given farther on, 'to a hatred of classical development whose beauty is only technical and can only interest the highbrows among us'.

This dislike for musical complication was constantly in evidence and was expressed and illustrated in a variety of ways. Monsieur Croche is, of course, extremely vehement when he touches the subject. He protests against an art that is 'almost incomprehensible', and addressing Debussy himself, or rather his fellow composers, he says: 'Would it not be well to suppress those superfluous complications whose ingenuity remind one of the lock of a safe? ... You are marking time because you know nothing but music and conform to barbaric and unknown laws.... Glorious epithets are showered on you, but you are merely cunning! Something half-way between a flunkey and a monkey.'

On another occasion Monsieur Croche similarly inveighed against 'intricacies that resemble those of a Byzantine locksmith'.

His articles in 'S.I.M.' were written at a time when Debussy was irritated by the attacks which a number of musicians directed against his own art, styling it 'Debussyst'. In these articles he repeats his condemnation of academic music in an exaggerated form, probably overstating his own convictions.

'Generally speaking,' he says, 'whenever a composer tries to complicate a form or an emotion in art, it is because he does not know what he wants to say.' Again he says, 'music becomes *difficult* when it does not exist, the word *difficult* being in this case only a screen to hide one's poverty. There is but one music, and it exists of its own right, whether it assumes the rhythm of a café-concert waltz or the imposing setting of a symphony. Why not admit that of the two good taste is often on the side of the waltz, while the symphony conceals with difficulty the pompous mass of its mediocrity.'

A whole series of axioms illuminate these articles of Debussy's. They are expressed sometimes seriously, sometimes in a bantering or mocking tone. He would probably have deemed it absurd for any one to make a serious attempt to classify them. But the attempt proves far from vain.

III

Musical Education. Composition and Form.

IN spite of his independence or perhaps because of it, Debussy's interest in the musical education of composers never flagged. The subject, indeed, caused him some concern, as may well be understood. As a pupil of the Paris Conservatoire, he had followed traditional lines until he won the highest reward—the Prix de Rome.

As a student and laureate of the Conservatoire, in the course of his study of the piano, harmony, counterpoint, fugue, and composition, and even during his sojourn at the Villa Medici, he had had ample opportunity of realizing the serious disadvantages of a conservative and unprogressive training. He saw the defects of an out-of-date system which blindly follows along old paths—be they good or bad—and takes its lessons from dead books rather than from life that is ever new. The natural reaction of his liberty-loving nature threw him into theories that were utterly opposed to those of his masters, or rather, professors.

His great ambition was to free musical education from the academic chains forged by the narrow traditions of German or Germanized pedagogues. How often was Debussy anathematized in the name of that tradition—*la Tradition*! It is evident in his articles that these attacks left a disagreeable impression on him and rankled in his mind: 'If ever a man of genius tries to shake off the heavy yoke of tradition, he is overwhelmed with ridicule. So the unfortunate man of genius decides to die young, and this is the only manifestation of his genius which is warmly encouraged.'

In a conversation with Monsieur Croche he remarks that some artists, musicians amongst them, have tried 'to shake off the old dust of tradition with the sole result that they were treated as symbolists and impressionists; convenient terms of contempt with which to damn them'.

His interlocutor, the advocate or interpreter whom he uses to voice his most caustic comments, replies: 'It is the journalists, the craftsmen who treat them thus. What does it matter? The germination of a beautiful idea appears ridiculous to these fools. Rest assured though, that there is greater hope of beauty in those who appear thus ridiculous than in the others—a flock of sheep meekly making for the slaughter-houses which a far-seeing destiny has prepared for them.'

Monsieur Croche stresses the fact that a musician must hold himself detached from every school, every clique, must 'remain individual . . . without blemish. . . . To my mind, the enthusiasm of a circle spoils an artist, for I dread his becoming eventually the mere expression of his circle. Discipline must be sought in freedom, and not in the formulas of a decayed philosophy which is of no value except to the weak. Take counsel of no man but of the passing wind, that tells us the story of the world. . . . Could there be anything more wonderful to contemplate than that a man should have remained unknown throughout the centuries until his secret is at last discovered by chance? . . . Oh, to have been such a man! . . . this is the only kind of glory worth while.'

The independent artist should never submit to the whims of fashion. Unfortunately he often does. Apropos of taste, Debussy wrote the following short chapter on hats: 'The thousand and one little customs to which a period conforms apply to every one. This is arbitrary; for more often than not they serve the purpose of but one individual. Let me illustrate this assertion by means of a rather trivial example: A man has a big head. After lengthy contemplation before his hatter's mirror he finds a shape which seems to him to make his head appear smaller. He decides on it—naturally enough. What is not so natural is that one then immediately sees people, who are not necessarily all fools, wearing hats that make them look ridiculous. That is a matter of fashion and not of taste, you will say. But this is not quite true; for fashion and taste are closely allied—or should be, at least. And if a man is willing to be ridiculous in his choice of a hat, there are excellent reasons for believing that this foolishness will extend to everything that is governed by taste—including music, the taste in which is most difficult to define. The chapter on "The relationship between hats and music" was overlooked by Carlyle in that compendium of cruel wit, his "Sartor Resartus". It deserves to be written, for the connexion is obvious and unquestionable. The hat of a lover of Symphonies is not the hat of an admirer of the "Damnation de

Faust". And the little soft felt that is easily rolled into a ball, ready for any emergency, cannot share the opinions of the shiny topper, glossy as a negro's skin. This latter demands of its owner a respectability which hampers enthusiasm whilst the little soft felt is untrammelled,—and can even throw itself at the orchestra's head as a last resort.'

Debussy himself affected a special shape in hats, and he disliked intensly to see young people copy this head-dress which he had evolved for his own use. He had no desire for imitators, for disciples. Above all, he abhorred those whose admiration for a master entails plagiarism: 'There is no school of Debussy! I have no disciples! I am I!'

The musician who, in spite of himself, became a Master made this brief declaration during the winter of 1910–11. He often repeated it; but in vain, for he could never rid himself of persistent disciples.

He not only objected to other composers taking credit for what was his, but he strove to rejuvenate his art, to modify his style. He refused to adhere to a particular genre of his own:

'In my opinion, to specialize is to narrow one's horizon until one is like those old horses who long ago turned the machinery for the merry-go-rounds and who died to the well-known strains of the "Marche Lorraine".' It seemed to him that a creator should display absolute independence, for his own sake as well as for the sake of others. He believed that a musician could never become a real artist so long as he remained a slave to the formula to which he owed his success. Some masters 'fought for a moment only, just long enough to win them a place in the market; but once the sale of their goods was assured, they quickly fell back, as though asking pardon of the public for having given it the trouble to admit them. They resolutely turn their backs on their youth. They stagnate in their success. They can never rise again to that glory which happily is reserved for those who, having devoted their lives to the discovery of a new world of ever-changing impressions and forms, end at last in the joyous conviction of having accomplished the true task. They have achieved success only at the *last performance*,—though *success* is indeed a vile word compared with the word *glory*.'

The following criticism of Saint-Saëns, who in his early days was 'full of enthusiasm and sought pure glory', is attributed to Monsieur Croche, who had on a previous occasion given it a different form: 'Though one may observe in some great men a stubborn determination to strike out on new lines, it is not so with many others, who obstinately repeat what had already brought success. Their skill leaves me indifferent. People call them masters. Might this not be a polite way of setting them aside or an apology for their lack of originality?'

Debussy does not consider ignorance of the past a necessary consequence of the essential quality of freedom. On the contrary, music 'has a Past whose ashes need stirring. For they contain the unextinguishable flame to which our Present must always owe a part of its splendour.' Above all, Frenchmen should know and study the old music of

France; for this is a happy, praiseworthy and fitting expression of that nationalism which, as will be seen, is at the root of the Debussyst doctrine.

The worst of it is that the study of old works tends to lead the musician to manufacture, so to speak, copies from the antique, whereas each period must possess its own peculiar art, harmonizing with everything else. The age of aeroplanes has a right to its own music. Every musician should create the forms necessary to the expression of his genius. He should not employ standard forms, however admirable may have been the masters who established them in other days, with different motives and without anticipating that they would become rigidly stereotyped.

Art must be spontaneous, music natural. What sometimes appears to be progress is in reality retrogression.

'There have been, and, the evils of civilization notwithstanding, there still are, certain charming little races that learned music as naturally as one learns to breathe. Their school of music is the eternal rhythm of the sea, the wind in the leaves and a thousand little noises that they eagerly listen to, without ever consulting standard text-books. Their only traditions are drawn from ancient songs mingled with dances, to which each one in his century added respectful contribution. The music of Java, however, is based on a counterpoint beside which that of Palestrina is child's play. And if, setting aside European prejudice, we listen to the charm of their percussion instruments, we are forced to admit that in comparison ours produce but the barbaric noise of a travelling circus. The Annamites perform a kind of embryo lyric drama which they owe to Chinese influence, and in which the tetralogical formula may be discerned. Only there are more gods and less scenery. . . . An excitable little clarinet directs the emotion. A tom-tom provides the note of terror . . . and that is all! There is no specially constructed theatre, no hidden orchestra. Only an instinctive need for art ingeniously satisfied; no trace of bad taste! And these people never thought of going to Munich in search of their formulas! What were they thinking of?'

We readily understand from these quotations why Debussy placed above any other the art of Mussorgsky, 'the art of an inquisitive savage who discovers music at every step made by his emotions', an art which avoids 'established forms, one might almost say official forms'. It is precisely all this official side of musical education, as opposed to the spontaneity we find in nature and true art, which needs modification in our schools of music—where the whole system of instruction is warped by a too rigid conventionality. It is impossible that the same educational procedure should suit everybody: 'For a long time past we have been so smitten with the mania for administration that it is applied to the most unlikely things in the world; and, naturally, this mania has now invaded the realms of art. When people wish to enjoy music they immediately found a society composed of such contradictory elements that they usually end by neutralizing one another. If any one wishes to study music, he can choose between the Conservatoire and the Schola Cantorum, where all must follow the same routine whether they have the genius of a Bach or the gifts of a Chopin. It is really inconceivable by what miraculous process the two words art and rule ever came to be associated. I do not suggest that the Choir Schools of the Renaissance should be revived, for they would hardly suit our own times. We might, however, seek inspiration from them and return to those open-air schools where the desire for immediate fame was unknown, and where the pupil bore the beautiful name of disciple, fearing his Master as much as he loved him. Do not let us confuse respect, which is a mere virtue, with art—that most beautiful of religions, built on love and egoism unashamed.'

A passing reference is made to one of the two very *administrative* Paris schools—the Schola Cantorum. Debussy attended only the concerts there, which in the space of a few years 'restored all the beauty of ancient music'. In 1903, at any rate, he speaks of it with approval as 'the nightmare of our National Conservatoire. Vincent d'Indy lectures on Composition; and his point of view is considered by some to be tainted with dogmatism. But his highmindedness and disinterestedness are universally admitted.' Later on, in 'S.I.M.', Debussy condemned indirectly, though not without bitterness, the excessive formalism of the school.

But his criticisms were chiefly directed against the Conservatoire—the school which he himself learned to know while studying there. These sometimes took the form of light sallies in which his animosity is nevertheless evident.

In 1903 a journalist discovered an infant prodigy, 'the Mozart of Saint-Maur'. Debussy, concerned 'to see so much fuss about so young a head', endeavours to dispel the father's twofold anxiety: 'M. Chagnon, the father, complains too that his son has not a good piano and that he can only attend at the Conservatoire once a week! . . . Both ills are easily remedied. Let his son stay away from the Conservatoire altogether. The money thus saved can be spent in buying a better piano. In this way he will combine utility and pleasure. (I do not know if I have made myself understood?)'

The Mozarts of Saint-Maur, the Bachs or the Rameaus of Paris and elsewhere should above all beware of the teaching of harmony at the Conservatoire. The method used is absurd. We do not even know the nature of the chords on which they claim to base their system. 'There is nothing more mysterious than a perfect chord. In spite of theories, ancient and modern, we are not at all sure, to begin with, that it is perfect or why another chord is condemned as imperfect or dissonant. Music should free itself as quickly as possible from the petty absurdities with which the Conservatoires try to hamper it.'

This theory, ripened by long reflection, was never abandoned by Debussy; not even when in February 1909 he was, to his own surprise, nominated to the 'Conseil supérieur d'enseignement' in place of Reyer who had just died. At the time a journalist asked his opinion of the school of which he would now be one of the technical councillors. He praised the instrumental classes, criticized the teaching of singing, and deplored the inadequacy of the teaching in solfège. His remarks, however, were prefaced by the following statement: 'The Conservatoire, in my opinion, is an institution where some subjects are excellently taught whilst others might be improved on. Thus, the teaching of harmony seems to me altogether faulty. I can assure you that I did very little when I attended the harmony classes. In my time the professors trained their pupils by means of a very futile little game which consists in discovering the "author's harmonization".[1] I humbly confess that I could never find the author's harmonization, and I was easily consoled for my failure.'

Such teaching, with its definite but shaky foundations, tends to stereotype composition, and to establish and propagate a superficial style. The use of free counterpoint is preferable: 'There is nothing one could more sincerely desire for French music', he wrote in 1902, 'than the suppression of the study of harmony as practised at school,—which is indeed the most pompously ridiculous method of assembling sounds. It has in addition this grave fault, that it standardizes composition to such a point that all musicians, with but few exceptions, harmonize in the same manner. You may be sure that old Bach, in whom is all music, snapped his fingers at harmonic formulas. He preferred to them the free play of sounds whose curves, parallel or contrary, produced

[1] i.e. the harmony given as model in the text-book used.

the wondrous efflorescence which adorns with imperishable beauty the least of his countless works. It was in the days of the *adorable arabesque*, and thus music conformed to laws of beauty inscribed in the whole movement of nature.'

Debussy frequently extolled the purely musical value of the arabesque, especially with regard to Bach.[1]

In the writing of music the quality of the chords is of less importance than their setting. Yet this is not taught in the school: 'For the sake of greater clearness, let us compare sounds to words. Everybody uses the same words. But whence comes the charm, the new light which these same words acquire when employed by some writers, if it is not from their particular setting? Similarly, how can we account for the unexpected charm of chords that are met with throughout music, if not by this fitness from the point of view of sound—which cannot be learnt, since nowhere is it visibly inscribed?

'Only the initiated sense it after consulting the seeming enigma of the masters. And often they make mistakes, and seek the cause of their emotions far from that quiet corner where, like the perfumed sweetness of violets among weeds, the sweetness of harmonies lies hidden.'

In this connexion Debussy must have had in mind his own experience, must have remembered the development of his own harmonic style and the lack of understanding shown by certain critics which sought to limit the magnificent creations of his

[1] See Chapter VIII of this volume, on foreign music.

genius to a few well-worn progressions of chords. Sometimes a veiled allusion may be guessed at, as in the article which he entitled 'Du Précurseur': 'As to music . . . its precursor was the first savage who took it into his head to beat two pieces of wood one against the other. One piece, being hollow, resounded, and tickled the savage fancy. 'Another shrewder savage stretched strings over the piece of hollow wood, scratched them with frenzied, ill-cut nails. . . . And this, without a doubt, was the origin of that chord of the ninth without preparation which subsequently so profoundly disturbed the musical world.'

In this same article in 'S.I.M.' he also appears to allude to the trivial influence of some humorous precursor which is supposed to have affected him: he remarks that 'a composer may unblushingly copy the forms employed in a classical work without surprising any one—this plagiarism will indeed earn for him congratulations—but let him employ a so-called "unknown" chord and lo! small-minded people raise their voices, crying "Stop thief!" Let me repeat that a chord in an edifice of sound has merely the importance of a stone in a building. Its real value depends on the place it occupies and the support it lends to the flexible curve of the melodic line."

Is it not possible that the Conservatoire—particularly the Prix de Rome, that supreme aim of its best pupils—may be partly responsible for the ills which afflict symphonic art? Debussy was convinced of it and repeatedly declared it to be so. The Prix de

Rome is reached by way of a Cantata, 'a hybrid form that partakes clumsily of all that is commonplace in opera or in the choral symphony. It is indeed an invention of the Institute—one of whose authorship no one need boast.' The pupils are trained on the Cantata course as a horse is trained for the Grand Prix. This 'superculture' alienates students from pure music, develops a taste for the theatre, and urges the laureates to set out on the libretto hunt immediately on their return from Rome. If there is so little pure music in France, it is thanks to the Prix de Rome: 'Had I a taste for statistics I could easily prove that no symphonic music, or very little of it, bears the official stamp.'

Chamber music, because of its very nature, 'requires a special process of transmutation to which your precious peace of mind must be sacrificed. It is difficult to sustain, and absolutely unproductive. Good-bye to the fine fat royalties and the flattering directorial handshake. You are now but an eccentric kind of savant, and your colleagues look at you with a contemptuous condescension begotten of success.'

Debussy never tired of condemning the Prix de Rome with its preliminary competitions and subsequent tasks. It was, he held, an absurd institution, which diverted laureates from the straight artistic path and put them on a level with prize cattle.' His observations, whether in the *Revue Blanche*, in *Gil Blas* or in *Musica*, were full of lively humour. He collected the chief points in his criticisms in the second chapter of 'Monsieur Croche'.

He recommended the suppression of all examinations and rewards which, he declared, would be better determined by 'the simple plan of drawing lots', instead of leaving their distribution to the incompetence of Jules Massenet in painting, or of W. Bouguereau in music.

He wished they would content themselves with presenting those most worthy of it with a certificate of higher studies and sending the laureates across Europe in search of a master or, 'should they succeed in finding such, an honest man who would teach them that Art is not necessarily limited to state-endowed institutions; that the love of Art must triumph over every illusion, every hardship, and must never be counted on as a road to fortune'.

Among the 'barbarous and unknown laws' to which, according to Monsieur Croche, musicians conform, and which liken them to 'something between a monkey and a flunkey', are the traditional rules of composition. To Debussy a form in music is like the head-dress which he treats of in his Chapter on Hats. It should be individual, created, or at all events adapted by each one for his own use. It has become a mere *passe-partout*, useful to composers who are wanting in genius,—like the Sonata pattern, for instance, particularly as it occurs in symphonies, which a certain school has slavishly imitated from ancient models.

Debussy does not hold with this exact reproduction of models from which wiser lessons should have been learnt: 'It seemed to me that the futility of the symphony had been established since

Beethoven's time. In the cases of Schumann and Mendelssohn it is but a respectful reproduction of the same forms weakened by repetition. The Ninth Symphony, nevertheless, was an inspired gesture, a magnificent desire for something grander, for greater freedom in accepted forms, while investing them with the harmonious proportions of a fresco. The true lesson Beethoven taught was not preservation of ancient forms or blind following in his early footsteps. Rather would he invite us to look through open windows to the clear sky. I fear these windows may have been closed for ever. The fact that genius has successfully handled this form of composition does not excuse the set and studied exercises that go by the name of symphony.'

The words 'set and studied exercises' were suggested to Debussy on hearing a long work by G. M. Witkowski which he subsequently criticized. In this connexion he describes an interesting experiment.

'The young Russian school endeavoured to invest the symphony with new life by taking themes from popular folk-tunes. They succeeded in producing sparkling jewels; but was there not an awkward disproportion between the theme and the developments which it was compelled to undergo? . . . Before long, however, the taste for folk-tunes spread over the entire musical world. From East to West, the smallest provinces were ransacked. From the lips of aged peasants ingenuous refrains were snatched, bewildered at finding themselves bedecked in harmonic trimmings. They took on an expression of sad restraint, but imperious counterpoint bade them forget their peaceful origin.' In these few amiably worded lines a cruel satire on a whole school of over-conventional symphonists is concentrated.

Although his conclusion takes the indecisive form of a question, its meaning is clear: 'Must we conclude that in spite of so many attempted transformations, the symphony belongs to the past with all its stiff elegance, its ceremonious arrangements, its sophisticated and painted audience? Is it not a fact that its ancient setting of faded gold has been replaced by the harsh brass of modern instrumentation?'

That this conclusion is inevitable becomes apparent in the next chapter, after a detailed examination of certain French symphonies, some purely and simply classical in form, as those of Saint-Saëns and Dubois—others cyclic, after the manner of César Franck and Vincent d'Indy.

If in music 'administrative' forms must be avoided in order to preserve the necessary independence, care should similarly be taken, whatever be the outward form of music, not to alienate its freedom by making it subservient to the theatre or literature. Music has an individual life—a rhythm of its own. It has nothing to gain by servitude, however glorious.

This recommendation may cause surprise, coming from the pen of a composer who set to music some beautiful literary and dramatic poems. It is, however, clearly stated, especially with regard to Bach, master of the 'free and adorable arabesque', in his opinions on Franck, writer of pure music, and in frequent declarations of war against the art of the theatre.

In the chapters which follow this exposition of the general principles on which Debussy's musical criticisms are based, examples will be found of the various reactions experienced by him as, in concert halls or theatres, he meets with French or foreign musical works.

IV

French Music and Nationalism.
Concert Music.

IT should not surprise us to find in a critic who cannot speak dispassionately of an art whose various manifestations he must take into account a very natural preference for the music of his country, and a brotherly friendship towards musicians who are his fellow-countrymen.

Most of Debussy's articles are animated by a very lively national feeling, a true nationalism, at once instinctive and reasoned, which he voices again and again in various forms but always with intense ardour. This enemy of all imitations of the classics, of all copies from the antique, repeatedly declared how necessary it was for the French to have a music of their own which, though modern, would not imply forgetfulness of the works of their old masters.

To his mind, art has little or nothing to gain by aiming at universality or cosmopolitanism. Every race is endowed with musical instinct, customs, forms and spiritual needs peculiar to itself. Frontiers are not purely geographical fictions. They exist, musically, in a very real way; and to try to abolish them would be as futile as it is idealistic.

'It is a mistake to believe that qualities peculiar to the genius of one race can be transmitted without injury to another—a mistake that has often harmed our music, for we are apt to adopt guilelessly formulas into which nothing French can enter. It would be better to compare these formulas with ours, to see what we lack and to endeavour to supply it without making any change in the rhythm of our thought. We should thus enrich our inheritance.'

Debussy did not believe in the possibility of a true international entente reaching beyond the frontiers of states, or at least of races.

When in 1910 a festival of French music was organized in Munich, in the most adverse conditions though with the best possible intentions, Debussy thus answered an inquiry:

'What business have we there? Have we been invited to go? No! Well, what is the meaning of this? It is quite evident that we have been more than hospitable to German musicians. What will remain of our present infatuation fifty years hence? We delight in everything that comes from outside. We clap our hands like children over a work that comes from afar—from Scandinavia; from the Germanic or the Latin countries—without gauging the true value and solidity of the work; without asking ourselves if our souls can really vibrate in sympathy with souls that are foreign to ours. We have reason to be thankful when we do not imitate, stammeringly, what these people say in their language; when we do not rhapsodize over false Italianism in music or false Ibsenism in literature and when some of our people do not make fools of themselves in their attempts to become exotic. There is no reason why the Germans should understand us. Neither should we try to absorb their ideas. Besides, though Munich may be well chosen from the political point of view, as the *Figaro* says, she cares nothing for our art. Concerts of modern music are only attended by a few music-lovers. People will go through politeness to hear French music. They will applaud, perhaps, with that Germanic courtesy that is so difficult to put up with. I am convinced that our art will not have made a single conquest in Germany. The event may perhaps be regarded as a means of bringing about a rapprochement by the propagation of our works! Music is not made for that . . . and the hour is ill chosen!'

On certain equally irritating occasions the musician's national sentiment bordered on Chauvinism. Debussy was undoubtedly proud of his country's qualities and he made no secret of the fact. When in 1909 he was questioned on his own musical history, he answered with this simple profession of faith: 'A musician must not be judged by his competitive work for the Prix de Rome. Since those days I have striven to eliminate by degrees all I had been taught. I have not tried to react against the influence of Wagner. I have simply allowed full play to my nature and temperament. Above all, I have tried to become French again. The French forget too easily the qualities of clearness and elegance peculiar to them and allow themselves to be influenced by the tedious and ponderous Teuton.'

National feeling such as his rejects not the knowledge, but the imitation of foreign art. This accounts for—and if need be excuses—the extravagance of certain opinions which appear farther on, particularly on Gluck and Wagner, both of whom are accused of having diverted French music from its natural path. For a tradition does exist, though all too many composers stray away from it and, swayed by various influences, follow in the wake of Germany.

Debussy aimed at re-establishing the continuity of this tradition, preaching in his articles on its importance and the necessity for its revival. And he sought to make of his works links with the art of other days, particularly the music of the sixteenth, seventeenth, and eighteenth centuries.

In his polyphonic settings of 'Trois Chansons de Charles d'Orléans' one may observe the influence of the music of the seventeenth century. Once only had he the opportunity of showing his appreciation of the work of two of his models—Claude Lejeune and Clement Jannequin. To the first he devoted a simple epithet on the subject of his 'delicious Madrigal'. In the case of the second, speaking of the 'Bataille de Marignan', he says that masterpiece 'is like the sound of the rude life of a camp, each cry, each noise of which is noted: the heavy trot of the horses mingles with the clear blast of trumpets in a secretly regulated tumult. It is so direct in form as to be almost folk-music, so exact is its picturesque transposition.'

Debussy loved Couperin, 'the most poetic of our clavecinists, whose tender melancholy is like an adorable echo issuing from the mysterious depths of landscapes where Watteau figures mourn'. It was his wish that we should draw from Couperin's art 'some lessons in wit and charm. We should do well to study the examples set us in certain little clavecin works by Couperin. They are exquisite models of a grace and spontaneity such as we no longer know. It is impossible to ignore the discreetly voluptuous perfume, the delicate perversity, half suggested, which innocently float around the "Barricades mystérieuses"....'

Farther on will be found his praise of Rameau, who composed for the theatre, and whom he loved to associate with Couperin and Watteau: 'Couperin and Rameau, these are truly French.... French music is all clearness, elegance; simple, natural declamation. The aim of French music is, before all, to please.... The musical genius of France may be described as a phantasy of the senses....'

Then, on another occasion, clearness and conciseness in expression and form were designated as the fundamental qualities of French art. This very rigid definition, which though acceptable is at the same time debatable, tends to place outside the national domain certain composers whose talent is not noted for these characteristics, and whose origin is, in some cases, foreign.

The beginning of the nineteenth century appears to be less sympathetic to him than the preceding periods. Debussy dwells on one name only of that period, that of Berlioz, a great artist who cannot be classified. 'Berlioz is an exception,—a monster. He is not a musician at all. He creates the illusion of music by means borrowed from literature and painting. Besides, there is, as far as I can see, little that is French in him.'

Debussy admires the power of his genius, but cannot like his purely musical qualities. The criticisms of his work are, nevertheless, free from prejudice. 'Because of his sense of colour and narration Berlioz was immediately adopted by painters. One can even say without irony that Berlioz has always been the favourite musician of those who are not very well versed in music. . . . The craftsmen are still scared by his harmonic liberties which they call clumsiness, and his devil-may-care form.'

As will be seen in the next chapter, Debussy disliked in Berlioz the musician who was too much addicted to the theatre. Nevertheless, he admired him as a symphonic composer. The real Berlioz should, he declares, be sought for 'in his purely symphonic music, or else in the "Enfance du Christ", which is perhaps his masterpiece, not excepting the "Symphonie Fantastique" and the music to "Roméo et Juliette"'.

At a time when the Concerts Colonne announced several times during the season, and always irrevocably, the last performance of the 'Damnation de Faust', he remarked: 'It will soon be easier to count the innumerable stars in the heavens than the last performances of the "Damnation de Faust" . . . and it would be less ridiculous.'

He sided warmly with Berlioz against unscrupulous producers when in Monte Carlo a musical adventurer wanted to transform the great work into an opera 'in which pantomime effects mingled with the attractions offered by the Folies-Bergères'. He described the 'Symphonie Fantastique' as 'ever that feverish masterpiece of romantic ardour which leaves one amazed that the music can interpret such extravagant situations without losing breath. Moreover, it affects one as would a battle of the elements.'

It was no doubt this work he had in mind when he whimsically declared: 'Berlioz fastens a romantic curl to old wigs.'

Debussy's principal grievance against the music of Berlioz had its origin in the fact that it was marred by an over-literary flavour. The romantic musician belongs to that class whose 'passion is satisfied with leaves which literature has dried between the pages of its books. Berlioz was content with it all his life. His genius found a bitter pleasure in airing its longings in an artificial flower shop.'

Though the genius of Berlioz shed its lustre over the whole of Europe, his influence on modern music has been negligible: 'In France it is only in Gustave Charpentier that a little of this influence is found, and there only in its decorative aspect; for Charpentier's art is undoubtedly individual as regards that which he wishes to express intimately in music.'

In the eyes of Debussy, Berlioz's chief merit lies in the freedom of his creative genius. He was incapable of accepting 'the wretched task of pandering to the public and encouraging its deliberate carelessness', in not having swelled the number of those manufacturers of music who deserve to be thus stigmatized: 'These artists fought for a moment only—just long enough to win them a place in the market. But once the sale of their goods was assured they quickly fell back, as though asking pardon of the public for the effort it had cost to admit them. They turn their backs resolutely on their youth; they stagnate in their success, and can never rise again to that glory which happily is reserved for those who, having devoted their lives to the discovery of a new world of ever-changing impressions and forms, end at last in the joyous conviction of having accomplished the true task. They have achieved success only at the *last performance*,—though *success* is indeed a vile word compared with the word *glory*.'

This theory, already quoted, was provoked by the conservative and reactionary continuity of the work of Camille Saint-Saëns. Saint-Saëns was one of the few French musicians on whom Debussy heaped scorn—adroitly administered though this was. Monsieur Croche is, of course, the mouthpiece for his severe censure of the illustrious master: 'I am sorry to find how difficult it is to retain one's respect for an artist who once was also full of enthusiasm and sought glory undefiled. I abhor sentimentality, Sir, but I wish I could forget that his name is Camille Saint-Saëns!' To which brutal words Debussy simply replies: 'Monsieur, I have heard his opera "Les Barbares".' Monsieur Croche continues 'with a degree of emotion I did not expect from him: "How could any one go so far astray? How could he forget that it was through him that Liszt's tumultuous genius came to be known and accepted? Has he forgotten his worship of old Bach? Why this unhealthy desire to write operas and pass from Louis Gallet to Victorien Sardou,[1] propagating the odious heresy that

[1] Writers of popular libretti.

one should *compose theatrical works* when this can never be reconciled with *composing music*?"' This conversation, the continuation of which will be found in the next chapter dealing with the theatre, appeared in the *Revue Blanche*. Debussy amended it slightly before republishing it two years later in *Gil Blas*.

The new version opens thus: 'Monsieur Croche, an old friend of mine, when speaking of M. Saint-Saëns, would gravely remove his hat and say in a faint, wheezy voice: "Saint-Saëns knows more about music than any other man in the whole world." Then, lighting a horrible little cigar, as black as a crow, he would continue: "His profound knowledge of music has, moreover, prevented him from ever subjecting it to his own personal desires. . . . Nevertheless we owe him our appreciation of Liszt's tumultuous genius; and he professed his worship of old Bach at a time when such an act of faith was also an act of courage. Let us then make no mistake. Saint-Saëns must be defined as the musician of tradition. He has accepted its aridity and enforced submission. He never allowed himself to go further than those whom he had chosen for his masters. This is marvellously shown in the 'Variations' for two pianos which he wrote on a theme of Beethoven's. That master's style is so faithfully copied, that one can only think of Beethoven. . . . I know of no more perfect example of disinterested respect! This devotion to form suggested symphonies which are models of logical development; and one asks oneself how he could ever have strayed so far as to find pleasure in *opera*, and pass from Louis Gallet to Victorien Sardou, thus propagating the odious heresy that one must *compose theatrical works*, as if this could ever be reconciled with the *composition of music*. . . ."' And Monsieur Croche repeats his regret at seeing Saint-Saëns thus lose 'the respect of all those young people who counted ardently on him to open up new paths to satisfy their longing for freedom and the open air.'

A harsh judgement indeed. Debussy realized its excesses. He explained and even excused it thus: 'The angry prejudice of Monsieur Croche would soften a little when he remembered the "Danse Macabre". He recalled with pleasure the hisses with which its first performance was received. One felt that he had really loved M. Saint-Saëns in other days, and that his vexation was due to the change in the latter which to him was nothing short of treason.'

There is even a slight trace of this annoyance in his brief praise of that same 'Danse Macabre', which this time appears over Debussy's own name: 'The attractive rhythm and timbre retain their peculiar vivacity throughout, and M. Saint-Saëns will forgive me if I venture to say that he showed in this work promise of becoming a very great musician.'

A very great musician. This title, denied to Saint-Saëns, was bestowed on another composer of French nationality—César Franck—at least with regard to certain aspects of his art. Not that his work is faultless: 'With Franck time was of no consequence; he was never bored. . . . Once he makes a good beginning there is nothing to fear, but sometimes he has difficulty in expressing his meaning. His genius spends itself in a curious and extremely complicated mixture interrupted by outbursts, pompous or dramatic, which he curtails, not through weakness, but because such methods were repugnant to his loyal simplicity.'

One of his principal works, the 'Beatitudes', 'is always music, is indeed always the same beautiful music'. Having heard part of it at the Concerts Lamoureux, Debussy devotes a half-feuilleton in *Gil Blas* to a criticism of the simple, pious composer: 'César Franck was a man devoid of malice, and the discovery of one beautiful harmony sufficed to make him happy for a whole day. On close examination, the "Beatitudes" proves to be a heterogeneous collection of ideas and truisms such as would daunt the stoutest heart. Only a sound, calm temperament like that of Franck could face it all with a smile on his lips—the kind smile of an apostle preaching the good word and saying: "Don't worry. God always knows his own." It is nevertheless with a curious impression that one hears Franck's very individual melody set to verses that would disgrace a mouth-organ. Much has been said of the genius of Franck without emphasizing the quality that was most peculiar to him, that is, his ingenuousness. This unhappy, misunderstood man had the soul of a child, a soul so irradicably good that he could dwell without bitterness on the unkindness of men and the perverseness of fate. Those choruses of his, too facile in their dramatic quality; the unrelieved monochrome of those developments, so tiresome and persistent, which sometimes appear to us to mar the beauty of the "Beatitudes", were written with a trustful candour that is truly admirable when he is in the presence of music before which he kneels murmuring the most profoundly human prayer that mortal ever breathed.'

The 'Beatitudes' had been performed at the Concerts Lamoureux after 'Rheingold'. And comparison with Wagner is inevitable. 'He never thinks evil, never suspects boredom. There is no trace in him of that trickery, so flagrant in Wagner, by means of which the latter rekindles the attention of a public weary of too continuous transcendency, by the introduction of some sentimental orchestral pirouette. Franck never flags in his devotion to music, and one must take it or leave it. No power on earth could make him interrupt a period which he believes to be justified and necessary. However long it may be, one has to put up with it. This is proof indeed of disinterested imagination, which tolerates no sob whose sincerity has not previously been tested.'

César Franck was, then, a pure musician: 'In this Franck is at one with the great musicians for whom sounds have a definite meaning in their sonorous acceptation. They employ them just for what they are, without ever asking of them more than they contain. And herein lies the great difference between the art of Wagner—beautiful, singular, impure, seductive—and the art of Franck, who is content to serve music, hardly asking for glory in return. What he borrows from life he repays to art with a modesty which even goes the length of anonymity. When Wagner borrows from life he dominates life, places his foot on it and obliges it to cry out the name of Wagner louder than the trumpets of Fame.'

This appreciation is free from the irony and humour so common in Debussy's criticisms. It is written with a solemnity worthy of the subject, in a tone that is almost religious. It is on this note too that he concludes: 'I should have liked to give a clearer impression of Franck, so that each one of my readers might carry away a lasting remembrance. It is well, amidst pressing preoccupations, to think of the great musicians, and above all to bring them to the thoughts of others. I have chosen to pay homage to one of the greatest on Good Friday, for I feel that this homage is in keeping with the idea of sacrifice evoked by the greatness of the man and the sanctity of the day.'

Franck, though French in heart and nationality, was not of French race. He introduced foreign elements into the music of his adopted country, elements which, to be more accurate, were indirectly Germanic in origin. 'César Franck is not French, he is a Belgian. Oh, yes, there is a Belgian school, and one of its most remarkable representatives after Franck is Lekeu, Lekeu the only musician who, to my knowledge, was influenced by Beethoven. The action of César Franck on French composers does not really amount to much: he taught them certain processes in composition, but their inspiration has no connexion with his.'

This theory, formulated in the course of a rapid interview, was clearly defined some years later when he was writing on Ernest Chausson. This composer, 'on whom the Flemish influence of César Franck weighed heavily, was one of the most delicate artists of our time. Though some contemporary musicians undoubtedly benefited by the influence of the Master of Liége, it seems to have had a bad effect on Chausson; for his natural gifts of elegance and clearness were in contrast with the sentimental rigour on which Franck's aesthetics is based.' Here occurs the nationalist declaration given at the beginning of this chapter, which shows the danger of the adoption by one country of the formulas peculiar to another. Some of Franck's faults are found in Chausson, 'who, nevertheless, manages to free himself and pursues a path that is entirely his own'.

His reflections on the art of Ernest Chausson were called forth by the 'Poème' for violin and orchestra which 'reflects his best qualities. His freedom of form never mars the harmony of its proportions. Nothing could be more touching than the exquisite poetry of the close when the music, abandoning everything in the nature of description or narrative, becomes the very sentiment that inspired the emotion. Such moments are precious in the work of an artist. In this case they are tinged with regret for the premature end which prevented his charming genius from accomplishing its complete evolution in works of delicate and ardent music.' Debussy also praised the 'Serres Chaudes' which this composer wrote on pieces by Maeterlinck: 'These melodies are little dramas whose passionate metaphysics Chausson brings out without overemphasis. One could wish that he had given more liberty to all that intimate emotion which vibrates in his very individual interpretation.'

Again, in 1903, Debussy wrote a critique of 'Quelques Danses', which Ernest Chausson had composed for the piano. His liking for these short pieces is not less evident: 'In the pieces entitled "Quelques Danses", we have a further example of Chausson's very individual style. One cannot help liking all these dances, but I must confess to a special partiality for the "Sarabande". Alas that on hearing it my emotion should be turned to pain by the thought that he is no longer with us, that we shall never see again the sincere kindness of his smile.'

The Germanic influence of the art of César Franck, if not definitely denounced, is at least commented on in dealing with the lengthy chamber music or orchestral sonatas written by his disciples, direct and indirect. All composers of Franckist symphonies are rapped on the knuckles, the critic administering the punishment with irony, kindness or bitterness, as the case demands. Debussy is surprised and pained to find young French composers anxious to fill with their often short and breathless inspirations the vast mould of the Beethoven sonata, whose futility, so it seemed to him, had long since been demonstrated.

In dealing with such composers as Paul de Wailly, a little-known pupil of César Franck who, needless to say, composed a symphony in three parts (which was given at the Société Nationale in March 1903), he confines himself to pin-pricks: 'This usually quadrangular form of music becomes triangular in the case of Paul de Wailly. . . . The title of symphony is so imposing that it intimidates one who has the audacity to assume responsibility for it. . . .' He gives a minute, emphatic and somewhat angry criticism of the performance of the works that J. Guy Ropartz or G. M. Witkowski built up on Breton folk-songs, whose stiff formality seems to fetter and stifle the personality of their authors.

It was in dealing with G. M. Witkowski's First Symphony in D minor that Debussy in 1901 indicted the modern orchestral sonata; and mention has already been made in the second chapter of this book of his merciless condemnation of these 'studied and stereotyped exercises' and 'copies from the antique'. The Lyonese composer was the first victim attacked (in April 1901) in Claude Debussy's first article as a musical critic. The critique is meant to be favourable, but there is at least one awful word in the harsh judgement on the slow movement of the great work: 'M. Witkowski's Symphony is built up on a Breton Chorale. In the first part we have the customary presentation of the theme on which the composer is about to work. Then begins the usual dislocation. . . . The second part may be said to have produced a vacuum. . . . The third part unbends a little in its Breton gaiety, with strongly sentimental passages here and there. Meanwhile the Breton chorale has retired—as is but proper—but it reappears and the dislocation continues. The specialists are visibly interested. They mop their brows whilst the audience calls for the author. . . . All the same, this is the best part. In it M. Witkowski is more spontaneous and more convincing. Besides, he undoubtedly has experience and shows no weakness, even when he is tedious. The voices he hears are authorized voices. It seems to me they prevent him from hearing another more intimate voice.'

Guy Ropartz is accorded an equally grudging and surly appreciation: 'The symphony on a Breton chorale has many of the qualities that make of Guy Ropartz a generous and energetic man. But why does he sometimes appear ill at ease and even stupefied? Is it perhaps due to the species of fascination which the word *symphony* exercises on contemporary musicians, so that their freedom of thought is crushed by the care they devote to form? By alternating movements, sometimes lively, sometimes slow, Ropartz has endeavoured to imbue with life that heavy block of marble which is a symphony; but this procedure immediately interferes with the unity of the composition. The first movement might be substituted for the last, and vice versa, for they are not in any way defined.'

As a lover of nature, Debussy had hoped to find local colour in this work; but despite the original Breton song, it has none: 'I must confess that the words "on a Breton chorale" had led my thoughts in a direction opposite to that which Guy Ropartz has given them. I beheld Brittany, the fitful wildness of the scenery, its harsh green sea more beautiful than any other, the Breton chorale—its soul, deeply religious, untamed, immutable as an old cathedral. And here I am presented with a little route map to enable me to follow the fantastic pranks of this same chorale. Great heavens! What do I care about the symphonic form? I know well what an admirable thing Guy Ropartz might have achieved had he not fancied himself obliged to extract a symphony from this Breton chorale which, when all is said and done, never did him any harm and for which, being as he is partly Breton, he should have a personal affection. I hope he will forgive me if I venture to teach him a lesson, he whose example is an education for all who are interested in music.'

At the beginning of his critique of this alleged Breton work of Guy Ropartz, Debussy had already railed against a certain custom at concerts where modern symphonies are performed: 'The audience is furnished with a thematic analysis, four pages long, with text and numerous examples. It is, indeed, just the sort of treatment a theme deserves; and the method of constructing a symphony is thus placed within the reach of all. What is to prevent a member of the audience with some little musical talent from being seized, on his return home, with the wicked desire to write a little symphony of his own and carry it forthwith, fresh baked, to M. Chevillard?[1] Thus the symphony in all its horror is encouraged. Besides, to my mind it is dangerous to initiate the profane into the secrets of the chemistry of music. Some members of the audience look at the aforementioned thematic analysis with as much awe as if it were an explosive; others regard it with bovine stupefaction. The more sensible use it as a fan, or they simply put it into their pockets; and herein lies the true moral of this story.'

Debussy considers it unnecessary cruelty to con-

[1] The conductor of the Concerts Lamoureux.

demn an unfortunate theme or an innocent melody to endless variations throughout a symphony or sonata. He could, however, write of it with humour, as in his critique of the 'Variations' which Rhené-Baton had carefully built up on a Breton song almost identical with that of G. M. Witkowski: 'Every one has seen the famous Scheffers, known as the Carpet Kings, in their audacious acrobatic feats. These include every possible way of climbing on another's back, of leaping dexterously across him, of transforming him into a kind of meteor rebounding on problematic shoulders. The "Variations" for piano and orchestra (written on an Aeolian theme by M. Rhené-Baton) remind one extraordinarily of these antics. The Aeolian theme bounds, leaps across, is multiplied, is amplified throughout the "Variations". Suddenly it reappears, to the satisfaction of the audience, and finally you find it again in the cloak-room, in the pocket of your overcoat.'

The affectation and grandiloquence of the modern symphonists, and their craze for complications that suggest the Byzantine locksmith, were never to Debussy's taste. On one occasion, however, he overcame his antipathy—when announcing the publication of the piano sonata composed by Paul Dukas. His friendship for the composer, stronger than his prejudice, prompted a warmly sympathetic article in which he went counter to his customary theories regarding music as a means of pleasure, and to his objection to excessive intellectuality in composition. Conscious of this denial of his principles, he submitted himself, three months later, to the invective of Monsieur Croche, who gives to the exaggerated praise its true value: 'You have', said the phantom to the critic, 'a tendency to stress unduly events that would have appeared natural, let us say, in Bach's time. You recently spoke of M. P. Dukas's sonata. He is no doubt a friend of yours—perhaps even a musical critic? Excellent reasons for speaking well of him. Your praise has, however, been surpassed; and M. Pierre Lalo, writing in *Le Temps*, in a feuilleton exclusively devoted to this sonata, with one stroke sacrificed in its favour those of Schumann and Chopin. . . .'

Debussy had praised Dukas in the warmest terms. His sonata was not written for the crowd, but was intended for 'those who really love music'. The former merely have a piano and breathlessly play certain pages over and over again. This is just as intoxicating as the *just, subtle, and mighty opium*, and it is a less exhausting way of creating happy moments. In this long work 'the restrained emotion interpreted and the unbroken sequence in the exposition of the ideas imperiously demanded a deep and intimate sympathy with the work. (This imperious quality is the hall-mark of M. Dukas's work, even when he deals in mere episodes.) It is achieved through intense patience in adjusting the parts which go to make up its structure; and it is to be feared that one could not easily follow its action at a concert performance. But that does not in any way take from its beauty or its poetry.'

Debussy is certainly aware that he is going to contradict himself, and he arms himself in advance against a contradiction that is as real as it is apparent: 'If the brain which conceived this sonata mingled the idea of construction with that of imagination, one must not conclude that the result is complication. Nothing could be more utterly absurd. M. P. Dukas knows what true music is. It is not merely a brilliant sonorous thing which pleases the ear to the point of satiety—(such a definition might easily, without straining the point, be applied to many types of music that are generally considered . . . very different). For him music is an inexhaustible treasure trove of images; and possibly of recollections which allow him to shape his ideas to the mould of his imagination. He is master of his emotion and does not allow it to run riot. Consequently he never permits himself those superfluous developments which so often mar the most beautiful things. In the third part of this sonata we find, beneath its picturesque exterior, a force which dominates its rhythmic fancy with the silent efficiency of steel mechanism. This force is the controlling element in the last piece, where the art of directing emotion is seen in all its power. One can even say that this emotion is constructive, invoking as it does a beauty akin to the lines of perfect architecture—lines which merge into and harmonize with the coloured vault of air and sky, joining with them in complete and perfect unison.'

Debussy then excuses himself for mentioning 'this rather unusual work', on the grounds of 'the place occupied by M. Dukas in contemporary art'. He declares that the sonata 'rises above ordinary experiments because of the lofty fidelity it exemplifies', and he concludes with this phrase whose ambiguity reveals his artistic leanings in spite ot himself: 'Music as Mussorgsky felt it or as Dukas and some others understood it is perhaps the only valid excuse for the title inscribed at the head of these notes.'

When the Société Nationale produced another work of Paul Dukas, his 'Variations' on a theme of Rameau's, Debussy again admired 'the proud mastery of his work'. But his love for Rameau restrained him: 'There are moments when Rameau himself would be hard put to it to discover his theme among such a mass of festoons and gilding. I believe Dukas only set himself to solve fleeting enigmas; but in reality he succeeds in solving weightier ones. Besides, one should see in the "Variations" only the curious play of the lines; and were I to sound my thought to its depth, I would confess that I prefer Dukas without Rameau.'

Unfortunately Debussy wrote but once of Gabriel Fauré, a master whose spontaneous grace formed a striking contrast to the intellectual force of the Franckists. It was in 1903, in an account of a concert given by the Société Nationale in the course of which was heard the 'Ballade' for piano and orchestra of that 'Master of Enchantments, Gabriel Fauré'. With impish gallantry he associates the composer and his interpreter. 'The "Ballade" ', he writes, 'is almost as lovely as Mme Hasselmans, the pianist. With a charming gesture she readjusted a shoulder strap which slipped down at every lively passage. Somehow an association of ideas was established in my mind between the charm of the afore-mentioned gesture and the music of Fauré. It is a fact, however, that the play of the graceful, fleeting lines described by Fauré's music may be compared to the gesture of a beautiful woman without either suffering by the comparison.'

Debussy wrote a few words on the subject of various other composers whose works he heard at concerts, among them Emmanuel Chabrier, Gustave Charpentier, Ernest Fanelli, and the young composers of ten or twenty years ago.

He devotes some ten lines to Chabrier, and deplores that this musician, 'so marvellously endowed by the comic muse', should have persisted in choosing subjects that were beyond his genius. He laments the fact that Chabrier 'died in the pursuit of lyrical drama—that Glucko-Wagnerian importation so foreign to our genius. In the "Marche Joyeuse" some of the melodies are masterpieces of imagination. This excellence they owe entirely to the music; and in this they differ from Offenbach, who usually gets his amusing effects from a distortion of the text—the music being relegated to a secondary place.'

In 1903 Charpentier was compared to Richard Strauss. 'The "Impressions d'Italie" are a voluptuous orgy of colour and rhythm. G. Charpentier's dreams are unlike those of R. Strauss, who also brought back with him "Impressions d'Italie". But in his rendering of impressions of the streets of Naples, Charpentier has no rival.' In 1912 he wrote of the same work in the following pleasant terms: 'Gustave Charpentier's "Impressions d'Italie" are a harmonious demonstration of the well-known axiom that youth is formed by travel. . . . In spite of the formalism of certain parts, one can sense already the perfume which is to emanate from "Louise" and the tumult of the crowd in that opera. The Institut, of which Gustave Charpentier has just been elected a member, should derive satisfaction from having sent to Rome a young man who so promptly organized his Italian impressions.' As we have already seen, this composer is the only one in France whom Debussy considered to have been influenced by Berlioz.

Ernest Fanelli, the precursor who on the memorable 17th of March 1912 attained glory that was subsequently extinguished, excited no enthusiasm in Debussy. On hearing the second part of the 'Tableaux Symphoniques' in 1913, Debussy wrote: 'At times he (Fanelli) too readily obeys the familiar spirit which prompts him to accumulate notes upon notes without much attention to balance. He has a very keen sense of decorative music, and this impels him to such minuteness of description that he loses himself and forgets how convincing his music might be if left to itself. May he receive the grace of contemplation. Life owes him that at least. Let us then in all sympathy have confidence in him.' It was in connexion with Fanelli and the Rust affair[1] that

[1] Fanelli was a composer suddenly 'discovered' by a few French periodicals. 'L'affaire Rust' refers to the discussion, which arose in Paris in 1912, on the garbling of F. W. Rust's (1739–96) music by his grandson, who wished to emphasize his importance as a precursor of Beethoven. (See M. D. Calvocoressi, *Principles and Methods of Musical Criticism*, pp. 78–9.)

Debussy wrote 'Du précurseur', a short chapter of aesthetics and history, the subject-matter of which has already been touched upon.

Among the French composers who were honoured by Debussy the critic with a short but flattering appreciation were Augusta Holmès, who at her death received the tribute of some twenty sympathetic lines; Augustin Savard, a former comrade of Debussy's in Rome, whose overture 'le Roi Lear' 'is too suggestive of Wagner for my taste', but 'gives evidence of fine musical qualities'; Louis Vierne, composer of a symphony for the organ, performed in 1903, in which 'the highest musicianship is allied to new and ingenious effects in the sonorous qualities peculiar to that instrument'; Jean Huré, whose 'Prélude Symphonique' of the same period appeared 'exceptionally forceful in form and above all finely orchestrated'; Gustave Samazeuilh, who also in 1903 had composed a Suite for piano, 'a work full of good-will but which appears to me not sufficiently matured'; Paul Pierné, the very skilful composer of a Symphonic Tryptich, 'De l'ombre à la lumière', for whom one could wish 'occasionally a less studied construction and greater emotional freedom'; Gabriel Grovlez, whose 'curious attempt at symphonic pantomime', the 'Vengeance des Fleurs', is a musical picture 'full of feeling and charm which, however, would need a stage setting, no matter how slight, to keep it within bounds'; Marc Delmas, composer of 'Deux Routes', 'a very youthful music, still reminiscent of the tests for the Prix de Rome'; Lily Boulanger, the first woman to win the Prix de Rome who 'is only nineteen years of age. . . . In her experience of the various methods of writing music, she is far older !'

In his desire for continual rejuvenation in composition for himself and his colleagues, Debussy never wearied in his attempts to divert French music into new channels. In the next chapter his prospectings in the domain of the theatre are dealt with. The future of the symphony also occupied his attention considerably. From the time of his début as a critic this anxiety was apparent; it was very marked in the last series of his articles—that is to say, from 1912 to 1914, during which period he very unwillingly played the role of leader of a school.

He was far from satisfied with the general outlook on the state of music in France. As early as 1903 he remarked that 'our period is somewhat over-ripe: indeed, greatly over-heated. We go from extreme complication to absolute nullity; we will on no account accept a leader (quite useless perhaps, but certainly a convenience). This is due to the fact that men of talent are numerous and men without talent countless—a circumstance which makes it difficult to choose that "objet de luxe" which enjoys such ardent predilection—"a great man". The fact is that we have not much confidence in ourselves, since we seek guidance from our neighbours across the frontier. What we need, what is indeed indispensable, is a young man of genius who will put things in order and revive our lost confidence. . . .'

When questioned in 1910 concerning the alleged renaissance of the classical idea, he admitted that he was doubtful though optimistic regarding French music of the future and indeed of to-day: 'Where have we anything in the way of joint action, general direction? In former times there were perhaps periods of discipline or what appear so to us from the distance, where individual efforts harmonized. But to-day! . . . Each one goes his way, seeks to develop his own personality—if he has one—or endeavours to imitate the personality of his neighbour, exaggerating it to the point of exasperation—and that is all. As for to-morrow, I do not know: who can foretell? Does the keen competition which creates such intense rivalry among artists portend the birth of a common ideal? Does it spell despair? Nothing of the sort. Music will come to life again. Let us work. Let us work, each of us according to his inspiration. The future will decide which works are classics.'

Debussy constantly deplored the fact that 'we seek guidance from our neighbours across the frontier'. Dealing with Gounod who 'escaped the imperious influence of Wagner', he compares French music after the death of Gounod and Bizet to 'a pretty widow who, having no one at hand to guide her, falls into the arms of strangers who do her injury'. He does not approve certain alliances: 'Like marriages of convenience, they end badly. . . .' During the war he went so far as to say: 'Why tire ourselves out writing symphonies and strain our muscles in vain? Why not write operettas? . . . Everybody cannot write *great* music (a term which has no definite meaning), but every one tries to. The result is a glut on the market, an abundance of so-called great Masters, and the notorious imbecility of current opinions on music.'

Many of his articles point the moral of simplicity: 'Let us purify our music. Let us free her from restraint. Let us beware of stifling music under an accumulation of redundant motifs and designs. How can we render her bloom or her strength while we are preoccupied with these details of composition? Why should we strive to maintain an impossible discipline in the swarming pack of little themes that elbow and override one another in their efforts to bite the legs of the unfortunate sentiment, which soon seeks safety in flight. As a general rule, whenever we produce complication of form or feeling in art, it is because we do not know what we mean.'

Debussy, therefore, was pleased to hear the Russians bring us 'new incentives to free us from ridiculous restraint. They will urge us to a better knowledge and a clearer hearing of ourselves.'

V

French Music (continuation)

The Old Theatre. Rameau and Gluck.

DRAMATIC art and music can never be made to harmonize. This maxim was dear to Debussy; and at least twice he gave expression to it, in the *Revue Blanche* and in *Gil Blas*, on both occasions in connexion with Saint-Saëns. The music of the theatre was to him a false and inferior type of art. He did not like it. Like all dramatic composers, he was aware of the extreme difficulty of reconciling music with the stage. Was it possible to arrive at a compromise between the two, to discover a *modus vivendi* which would allow the drama or the poem and the symphony to exist side by side in harmony? Must not one or other perforce be sacrificed? 'It is always the vexed question whether music is to be the master or the slave.' It was Debussy's wish that music 'should reign supreme'. He likewise objected to music being taken in tow by foreigners, whether in the realm of the theatre or in that of the symphony.

In 1911 Debussy's love of pure music prompted him to make surprising statements regarding the relations between music and verse. He had composed a number of songs, some of which will live as masterpieces—models of the perfect adaptation of music to beautiful poems. This personal experience did not prevent his deploring the craze of certain composers for setting to music poems that might well be left alone. In his opinion even the best musicians, even Schumann, great master of the 'Lied', fail to understand the poetry on which they are working: 'Strictly speaking, really beautiful poems are not so plentiful. Is there any one writing them to-day? When one does find them, it is better to leave them alone. The full, classical verse of Henri de Régnier cannot be set to music. And could any one imagine music to the poetry of Racine or Corneille? But nowadays young composers are not content unless they see famous signatures beside their own. In any case, of what use are poems to music? It is more common to find beautiful music set to bad poems than bad music to real poetry.'

Having made these frank statements, Debussy repeats a frequently cited theory of Lamartine; and taking the stage himself, he writes: 'True verse has a rhythm of its own which is, if anything, a hindrance to us. For instance, I recently set to music—I don't know why—three ballads of Villon. . . . Yes, I do know why. It was because I had for a long time wanted to do so. Well, it is very difficult to follow; to mould the rhythm satisfactorily whilst keeping to one's own inspiration. If it is a case of manufacturing, if one is satisfied with a work of juxtaposition, obviously it is not difficult; but neither is it worth while. Classical verse has a life of its own, a dynamic force, to quote the Germans, which has nothing to do with us.' Debussy comes to the conclusion that the composer should himself write the poems he would use and should note them down, not in verse, but in rhythmic prose.

This eternal disagreement of music and poetry, to which Debussy was evidently very sensitive, contributed to his dislike for dramatic works; and one must not be surprised at the unfailing severity of his criticism of all operas. The constant subjection of the music to the drama as well as to the spectacle, the ceaseless disagreement between poetic and musical rhythm which inevitably pained him, were to him defects which made the writing of a good opera an utter impossibility. These considerations led him to a severity of criticism bordering on injustice, of which we have numerous examples.

He professes disdain and even contempt for most of the dramatic attempts of his colleagues who degraded music to the service of the theatre, imitated alien dramatists, and wrongfully adapted one to another elements that with difficulty blend. Notwithstanding this, however, he never tires of referring in terms of the warmest admiration and affection to an old French musician—Rameau—who, in a genre essentially national, conscientiously served music. This great musician composed for our Opera 'ballets avec chant', a form that was peculiar to France but which we have allowed to fall into disuse. He is, in addition, 'a musician of old France who, whilst obligingly adding to the charm of the spectacle, surrenders none of his rights as a composer'.

In 1908 the Opera House announced the revival of 'Hyppolyte et Aricie', a work which for more than a century had been consigned to oblivion. Debussy feared that it might be misunderstood and that this very French type of art, so old and so far removed from modern tastes and customs, might not be received with the deep and lively sympathy it merited. 'We have', he says, 'adopted a frenzied method of shaking up the orchestra as one mixes a salad. While this continues we must give up all hope of producing music. The beauty of this frenzy is so obscure that it is difficult to see it at all. I fear our ears have lost the faculty of listening with delicate attention to music such as this, which precludes all unpleasing noise, but which welcomes with charming courtesy those who know how to listen to it. It would be a pity if we had forgotten these manners that once were ours and if we should respond to them as though we were barbarians. We need not fear to be too respectful or too deeply moved. Let us listen to the heart of Rameau. Never was voice heard at the Opera more French than his.'

Is it not surprising that although there was a Bach Society in Paris there had not previously been a Rameau Society? 'The latter is our blood ancestor; we surely owe this tribute to his spirit.' Dealing with Couperin, with whom he associates him, our critic recalls the memory of Watteau: 'Rameau met with much the same fate as Watteau. The latter dies; years pass; a silence falls . . . organized by colleagues who knew what they were about. Now the light of glory shines full on Watteau's name and no proud period of painting can make us forget the greatest, the most moving genius of the eighteenth century. In Rameau we have the perfect counterpart of Watteau. Is it not high time that he were admitted to the place that is his by right, instead of forcing

French music to model itself on clumsy cosmopolitan traditions that prevent its natural genius from developing freely?' Our craze for things foreign has made us forget our great musician: 'To many people Rameau is the composer of the famous rigodon from "Dardanus", and that is all. . . . This is indeed an instance of that sentimentality peculiar to the French people, which moves them to adopt with frenzy formulas of art as well as forms of dress that are not in keeping with the spirit of the soil.'

Debussy heard several of the works of Rameau at concerts or at the theatre: he wrote of them all with the same enthusiasm. He first heard at the Schola the two first acts of 'Castor et Pollux', conducted by Charles Bordes, and wrote the following detailed account of it: '. . . After an overture, a noise designed to allow the pannier dresses to spread out their silken folds, the chorus raises its voice in lamentation at the funeral rites of Castor. One is immediately enveloped in an atmosphere of tragedy which, however, remains human; that is to say, there is no suggestion of the peplum or the helmet. They are simply people who weep as you and I weep. Then appears Télaïre, who loved Castor, and we hear the gentlest, deepest complaint that ever issued from a loving heart. Pollux enters, leading the combatants. They have avenged the insult to Castor; then the chorus, and a warlike diversion, a movement of superb strength, pierced now and then by the blast of trumpets, brings the first act to a close.'

In the second act, among other marvels, is 'the monologue of Pollux, "Nature, amour, qui partagez mon sort", so individual in accent, so novel in construction that time and space are lost and Rameau becomes a contemporary to whom we shall express our admiration at the conclusion.' Debussy would like to mention everything. Here is the last scene of this act: 'Hebe dances at the head of the Heavenly Pleasures who hold in their hands garlands of flowers with which to enchain Pollux. Jupiter ordained the magic spell to snatch Pollux from his desire for death. Never was a feeling of calm, peaceful voluptuousness so perfectly interpreted. The luminous play in the supernatural atmosphere is so wonderful, that Pollux needs all his Spartan strength to escape from its enchantment and remember Castor (whom I had forgotten for quite a while). In conclusion I should like to give some idea of all the delicate elegance of this music, so free from affectation and from the contortions of questionable graces. Have we set up in its stead a taste for mere prettiness or the intricacies of a Byzantine locksmith?'

Debussy makes excuses for the length of this feuilleton devoted to 'a subject which, perhaps, lacks present-day interest'. His excuses are: 'In the first place, Rameau, who was worth it; secondly, moments of real joy are rare in life, and I did not wish to be selfish and keep these to myself.'

In 'Hippolyte et Aricie', despite the extreme poverty of the libretto which called into play 'Rameau's prodigious inventive powers', Debussy is enchanted with the entrances, the choruses, the dances, and the symphonies. In an article written to precede the first performance, he remarks on the qualities of this score, qualities no longer possessed by modern composers of opera: 'It is indeed a pity that we should have lost this charming style of music, as utterly as we have lost all trace of Couperin. It was free from redundancy and full of wit. Now we are almost afraid to be witty lest we should thereby lose in dignity, in the pursuit of which we wear ourselves out,—often without success. Where is the flexible subtlety that so well became the sounds of our beautiful language? We shall find it again in this "Hippolyte et Aricie" of 1733 which the Opera is about to produce in 1908. In spite of the sad reproach suggested by these two dates thus coupled, we may be sure that if the setting has faded, the expression has remained intact, so just and fitting is it. For in this it resembles all things whose beauty is eternal—despite the unjust forgetfulness of men, they can never really die.'

On this occasion the theory regarding nature, so dear to the composer-critic, is again stated, together with his nationalist principles: 'Why have we not followed the good advice he gave us to observe nature before attempting to describe it? Perhaps we have no time nowadays? And our music blindly follows in the wake of "faits-divers" from Italy, or legendary tales—crumbs that fall from the Tetralogical table d'hôte. We ignore the "ballet avec chant" which was ours by right of the definite examples left by Rameau. Although Russia has taken it from us, it was infinitely better suited to certain sides of our character; it only required to be handled with some regard for elegance.'

The days of Rameau were, in Debussy's judgement, among the most glorious in the history of music in France. Yet, even their memory had almost been lost. 'There was one great French epoch,—the eighteenth century,—the days of Rameau. To how many hostile influences must this tradition, then in its infancy, have been obliged to yield? First came Gluckism, which, a long way ahead, paved the way for Wagnerism. After that, Rossini, leaving few traces; then, of much more importance, Meyerbeer, whose influence is too little known although it is apparent to-day in the work of many composers. Finally Wagner, who was revealed to us thirty years too late.' This statement was made in 1910 to a reporter of *Paris-Journal.* Already in 1903 Debussy had tried to account for the inexplicable phenomenon of the neglect of Rameau. He saw in it 'a mystery frequently occurring in the history of art, which can only be explained, perhaps, by the strange and arbitrary chain of historical events....'

In explanation thereof, Debussy systematically opposed to Rameau, the true Frenchman, the German musician, Gluck, who usurped his colleague's place. According to him, Gluck was the hereditary enemy who broke through our national tradition and destroyed our music. This foreigner is harshly criticized on several occasions, and always to Rameau's advantage: 'Gluck's influence on French music is well known. This influence could never have asserted itself but for the intervention of the Dauphine, Marie-Antoinette (an Austrian). This reminds one that Wagner owed the production of

"Tannhäuser" in Paris to the influence of Mme de Metternich (an Austrian). Nevertheless, the genius of Gluck is deeply rooted in the work of Rameau. "Castor et Pollux" contains, in curtailed form, the first sketches which Gluck subsequently developed. Interesting comparisons can be made which prove that if Gluck had usurped the place that should be Rameau's on the French stage, he did so only by assimilating and appropriating the latter's beautiful ideas. What has kept the Gluck tradition alive? The pompous and unreal method of treating the recitative should condemn it were there not, besides, the habit of rudely interrupting the action, as does Orpheus when he has lost his Eurydice, with a romance which does not exactly indicate a lamentable state of mind. . . . But it is Gluck! . . . and therefore is accepted. As for Rameau, it was his own fault. He should have become naturalized!'

The same central idea regarding Gluck and the same association of Gluck and Wagner occur in the article on 'Hippolyte et Aricie': 'Queen Marie-Antoinette, who always remained an Austrian—a sentiment for which she was made to pay once and for all—imposed Gluck on French taste. Thus our beautiful traditions became warped, our desire for clarity stifled, and via Meyerbeer, we arrived quite logically at Richard Wagner.'

This invective found formal expression one day. It was in 1903, in the Open Letter to Monsieur le Chevalier W. Gluck. Debussy wrote it when 'Iphigénie en Aulide' was revived at the Opera. Close on fifteen years later he republished it in

'Monsieur Croche, antidilettante', keeping to the original text. It was therefore no sudden whim but a ripe opinion, formally expressed.

The second part of this letter is an account of the revival, and most of it is devoted to praise of the prima donna, Rose Caron. The first part opens thus impertinently: 'Monsieur, shall I write to you or call up your spirit? My letter will probably not reach you, and I doubt that you would consent to leave the abode of happy shades to come and talk with me of the future of an art in which you excelled sufficiently to wish to be left outside discussions that trouble it unceasingly. I shall therefore write to you and evoke you alternately, and thus endow you with an imaginary life which will allow me a certain degree of licence. Please forgive me if I do not admire your works. I am none the less mindful of the respect due to so illustrious a man as you. . . .'

Gluck's life in aristocratic circles is first recalled with irony: 'You were a Court Musician. Royal hands turned the pages of your manuscripts and bent on you the approbation of a painted smile. They rather plagued you, it is true, on the subject of one Piccini who wrote more than sixty operas. In this you conformed to a common law which ordains that quantity must usurp the place of quality, and that the Italians should in all ages overstock the music market. The aforementioned Piccini is so entirely forgotten to-day that he was driven to take the name of Puccini in order to be performed at the Opéra-Comique. In any case, those discussions between elegantly learned abbés and dogmatic encyclopedists can hardly have interested you much. Both showed in their discussion of music an incompetence which you would find equalled in our world to-day. And if you did show independence by conducting the first performance of "Iphigénie en Aulide" without your wig and wearing a nightcap, your chief anxiety was to please your king and your queen. But your association with these mighty ones has stamped itself on your music, giving it an aspect of almost uniform pompousness. If love is introduced, it is with majestic decency; and even suffering drops preliminary curtsys. . . . Whether it be more elegant to please King Louis XVI than the people of the Third Republic is a question which your condition of dead man prevents me from answering in the affirmative.'

Debussy's apparent desire to popularize the lyric theatre is not untinged with irony. For he too, despite his humble birth, was an aristocrat: 'Your art', he goes on, 'was therefore essentially one of pomp and ceremony. The common people only shared it from afar. . . . They watched the others (those who were happy . . . satisfied!) pass by. You were to them, so to speak, the wall behind which something happens. We have changed all that, Monsieur le Chevalier: we have democratic tendencies and we want to reach the heart of the masses. Things are none the better for that, and we are none the prouder! (You have no idea how hard we find it to found a popular Opera).'

This general critique concluded, Debussy admits that 'in spite of its aspect of luxury', the Chevalier's art exercised great influence on French music: 'One recognizes you first of all in Spontini, Lesueur, Méhul, &c. . . .; you contain the germs of Wagnerian formulas, and this is unbearable (you will see why later on).' And so criticisms crowd on one another and accumulate as Rameau, the true Frenchman, the pure musician, is evoked: 'Between ourselves, your prosody was very bad: at least, you turn the French language into an accentuated language when it is, on the contrary, a language of fine shades. (I know . . . you are German.) Rameau, who helped to form your genius, has examples of fine vigorous declamation which should have been of more service to you. Out of respect for your feelings, I refrain from speaking of Rameau as a musician—that would be too unkind to you. It is thanks to you, too, that the action in drama has been allowed to take precedence of the music. . . . Is that altogether admirable? On the whole, I prefer Mozart, who, good man, ignored you completely and troubled himself only about music. In order to facilitate this tendency to make the action predominate you have recourse to Greek themes. These have furnished people with an opportunity for talking the most arrant nonsense about the alleged relation between your music and Greek art. Rameau was infinitely more Greek than you, (don't get angry, I shall soon have done with you). More than that, Rameau was lyrical, which suited us from every point of view. We should have remained lyrical without waiting through a century to become so again.'

Again we have the great reproach of nationalism

and the associating of Gluck with Wagner: 'It is thanks to your influence that French music enjoyed the unlooked-for advantage of falling into the arms of Wagner. I am convinced that without you, not only would this not have happened, but French musical art would not have inquired the way so often of persons who were only too anxious to lead her astray. Lastly, you have benefited by varied and false interpretations of the word "classical": the fact that you invented that dramatic drone which permits the suppression of all music is not sufficient to earn for you this classification, and Rameau has a better claim to be so called. . . .'

Here we have proceedings instituted with an entire lack of impartiality; charges made without leniency; and a biased judgement. His prejudice becomes glaring in his account of the interpretation: 'Your death is to be regretted for the sake of Mme Caron. She made of your Iphigénie a figure full of purity, infinitely more Greek than your conception. . . . She discovered for herself all the inner feeling you failed to put into the role. . . . With this woman your music becomes immaterialized, it can no longer be labelled as of a definite period: for thanks to a gift which makes one believe in the survival of the ancient gods, she possesses that sense of tragedy which can lift the black veil of the past and bring to life those dead cities where the cult of Beauty was harmoniously allied to that of Art. . . .' Briefly, of all the emotion that the critic had experienced during the performance, nothing was due to Gluck himself. The exaggeration is obvious; it is the outcome of intense reaction against the unjust contempt with which Rameau's magnificent art was treated and the immolation of our old French Master on the altar of his foreign successor. Our love for all that is alien is unceasingly carried to such excesses that one can forgive those who go to the other extreme in just defence and championship of an admirable musician of our race.

VI

French Music (continuation and conclusion): The Theatre in the Nineteenth and Twentieth Centuries.

DEBUSSY felt very keenly the necessity for the predominance of music over the scenic elements—a predominance maintained by Rameau but abandoned by Gluck. He was consequently incapable of appreciating the greater number of operas, comic operas, tragedies in the Wagnerian style, lyrical dramas, 'during which all hope of music must be completely abandoned'. If we look through the lyrical history of France during the nineteenth century, or turn over the pages of the repertory of our Opera, we find hardly anything that has not been anathematized by the intolerant critic.

One day, in speaking of the 'Petite Maison' by W. Chaumet, a work which was out of date even when it made its appearance at the Opéra-Comique in 1903, Debussy recalled in harsh terms the years round about 1840, 'that disastrous period which witnessed the glory of Adolphe Adam and the famous mediocrity—if I may so express myself—of that other musician, Clapisson! . . .' The masterpiece of that time, which is also a masterpiece of what is known as French Opera—namely, Meyerbeer's great opera, is looked upon by him as a sort of musical calamity: 'The Huguenots' 'is one of our little daily trials. . . . This opera is one of the most tiring to listen to and even to perform; the music is so strained that even the anxiety to massacre unfortunate Protestants does not altogether excuse it. Then, how pleasant it must be for those in the audience (the Protestants), for there are certainly some left. Moreover, in spite of Meyerbeer's genius, I cannot approve of gunshots as orchestral effects. Let us say no more lest "la Juive" be dragged from a well-deserved oblivion, or perhaps some one gives us an opera on the expulsion of the religious orders. Such things are, perhaps, necessary; and as that delightful dyspeptic, Carlyle, said: " . . . but for Evil there were no Good, as Victory is only possible by battle".'

Meyerbeer's famous work, which has been popular for close on a hundred years, had, so he thought, served as model to another Berlin Jew—Offenbach, 'whose strange genius was a compound of a special hatred of music and transcendental irony'. In support of this theory Debussy declares that the power of the false, bombastic art of Meyerbeer, with its unconscious buffoonery, 'lies in its ungainly rhythm and the comic effects achieved by a frenzied repetition of one syllable in a line'. Offenbach was, so Debussy suggests, content to exploit these grotesque elements which his glorious fellow-countryman had unwittingly brought together: 'If the Calvinist song in "The Huguenots" (in which the warlike qualities of M. de Coligny are extolled by truculent bass voices that gargle whilst they noisily repeat "Vive Coligny!") is compared with the air which marks the entrance of Paris in the third act of "La Belle

Hélène", many curious points of comparison will be found. Why is the first considered great music and the second "opéra bouffe"? '[1]

A famous French musician, Berlioz, finds himself unexpectedly associated with these two foreigners, Meyerbeer and Gluck, both of whom were inimical to French music: '. . . Properly speaking, Berlioz was never a musician of the theatre. There is real beauty in "Les Troyens", a lyrical tragedy in two parts; but owing to its defects of proportion it is difficult to perform, and the effect produced is monotonous, not to say tedious. . . . Besides, Berlioz puts nothing original into it. It is reminiscent of Gluck, whom he passionately loved, and Meyerbeer, whom he cordially detested. No, that is not where Berlioz is to be found.' We saw in the preceding chapter where Debussy recognized the genius of his colleague.

His profound dislike of traditional opera and theatrical music in general is much in evidence in an article in the *Revue Blanche* devoted to 'a very curious institution situated in the Place de l'Opéra'. This institution is none other than our great lyric theatre, or museum or conservatoire of French art,

[1] Debussy once had occasion to write an account of 'Sire de Vergy', an operetta by Claude Terrasse. He praised its brightness, its musical skill, its clever orchestration, and concluded his article with the following sally: 'People should go to it, and encourage MM. de Caillavet, R. de Flers, C. Terrasse, in their attempt at opéra bouffe, if only for the sake of discouraging . . . the other opera, which is neither bouffe nor opera but a species of microbe whose nefarious ravages must be sternly combated.'

which rejoices in the pompous name of The National Academy of Music and Dancing. It is, perhaps, too caustic a satire on the repertoire offered by the Opera of Paris, and the manner in which it is presented.

In this Opera, the outside of which, according to Debussy, resembles a railway station and the inside Turkish Baths, 'they keep on making a strange noise which the people who have paid for it call music. . . . One must not altogether believe them. Thanks to special privileges and State endowment, anything may be produced at this theatre. It matters so little, that the boxes are provided with ante-rooms installed with carefully-thought-out luxury. In these one may sit in comfort, hearing nothing of the music: they are the last salons where conversation is still indulged in.' The critic, whilst deploring this state of things, realizes the impossibility of overthrowing 'a solid wall of headstrong officialdom through which no searchlight can penetrate'. A change in the administrative customs of the great institution could only be brought about by revolution or fire.

In spite of his anti-Wagnerism, Debussy expresses surprise in 1901 that 'the studied apathy of this place' has not yet been shaken off and the works of Richard Wagner produced: 'Should we not long since have become acquainted with the entire Tetralogy? For one thing, we should thus be rid of it, and the Bayreuth pilgrims would cease to annoy us with their German gasconades. . . . They did well to produce the "Meistersinger" at the Opera; it would have been even better to give "Tristan and Isolde" (in which Chopin's charming soul appears, reflected here and there in the music directing its passion). There remained only "Parsifal" to fear; and for family and mercenary reasons, Mme Cosima Wagner reserves, in this case, the right of production to herself.'

What is played in our great national theatre? First and foremost 'Faust'. Debussy, far from showing surprise at this or complaining, finds it quite natural and undertakes the defence if not the panegyric of Gounod and his masterpiece: 'Many unprejudiced people—that is to say, people who are not musicians—ask themselves why they persist in producing "Faust". There are many reasons, the best being that Gounod's art represents a phase in French feeling. Whether we like it or not, such things are not forgotten.'

One soon realizes that though Debussy may like Gounod principally for his own sake, this liking is not altogether unconnected with his opposition to the great enemy of French music—Wagner. From the outset of his article he contrasts the two composers, and on purely dramatic ground: 'With regard to "Faust", eminent writers on music have reproached Gounod with having travestied Goethe's thought. It has not occurred to these same eminent personages that Wagner may have distorted the character of Tannhäuser, who, in the legend, is not at all the good, repentant little boy that Wagner makes him, and whose staff, burnt by the memory of Venus, never flowered again. For taking this liberty Gounod, being French, may be forgiven; but it is inexcusable in the case of Tannhäuser and Wagner, both of them German.'

In praising Gounod, Debussy sets up a parallel between him and the German master: 'Though Gounod may not achieve so harmonious a curve as one might desire, he deserves praise for having escaped from the imperious genius of Wagner—whose wholly German concept is not very clearly justified in the fusion of arts which he aimed at, and which is now nothing more than a formula for attracting customers.'

In deciding the true position occupied by Gounod in the history of the art, Debussy again refers to the other enemy, Gluck: 'Gounod, in spite of his failings, is necessary. To begin with, he is cultured; he knows Palestrina, collaborates with Bach. He is sufficiently far-seeing in his respect for tradition not to acclaim the name of Gluck—another foreign influence, inaccurately gauged. Rather does he encourage young people to love Mozart; this shows his disinterestedness, for he never sought inspiration from him. His relations with Mendelssohn were more transparent, since he owes to him that method of developing the melody in sequences which is so convenient when one is not in the mood. (This influence is indeed perhaps more direct than that of Schumann.) Moreover, Gounod makes room for Bizet, and that is well. Unfortunately, the latter died too soon; and although he left one masterpiece, the future of French music remained problematic....'

The conclusion is most favourable to Gounod: 'Let us set aside dogmatic severity and take the opportunity of respectfully greeting his name. A man may live in the memory of his fellows for a variety of reasons, and these need not always be weighty. One of the surest is to have aroused emotion in a large number of his contemporaries. No one will dream of denying that Gounod gave himself generously to this.'

Reyer, Saint-Saëns, and Massenet are also still performed at the Opera. Debussy accounts for the success of the first in terms of fierce contempt: 'There are people who view a landscape with as much interest as would a cow. Such people listen to music with cotton-wool in their ears.' Saint-Saëns and Massenet are dealt with at greater length, the former with severity, the latter with sympathy.

We are already acquainted with Debussy's general opinion of Saint-Saëns, or rather, the opinion of the uncompromising Monsieur Croche. This fertile musician, in his role of dramatist, was judged without the least attempt at impartiality, and the verdict was passed on from the *Revue Blanche* to *Gil Blas* in practically identical terms. Here is the brief conversation in which was assailed this too respectful inheritor of accepted forms who 'strayed so far as to take pleasure in opera and fall from Louis Gallet to Victorien Sardou, thus spreading the abominable heresy that one should write drama, when this can never agree with writing music'.

Monsieur Croche says: 'Surely the Almighty in His liberality had placed innumerable opera-makers on earth! Saint-Saëns was not needed to swell their numbers. Moreover, his example could only encourage their odious trade, and it is a pity. . . . How did he fail to see, that he thereby forfeited at one stroke the respect of all those young people, who confidently relied on him to open up new paths to their desire for freedom and fresh air? . . .'

Speaking with a depth of feeling that is rare in this satirical old phantom, Monsieur Croche continues the diatribe prompted by disillusioned admiration: 'I have a horror of sentimentality, sir, but I should like to forget that he who wrote "Les Barbares" is called Camille Saint-Saëns.' In vain Debussy ventures on a timid objection: 'But is "Les Barbares" worse than many other operas which you do not mention, and must we on its account lose for ever the memory of what Saint-Saëns once was?' Monsieur Croche brusquely interrupts: 'That opera is a bad example because it comes from great heights. . . . Saint-Saëns owed it to himself, and still more to music, not to write this rubbish which contains formulas contradictory to his spirit. There is even a farandole in it whose archaic perfume has been praised with that barefaced ignorance peculiar to the great musical critics. It is at best a faded echo of the exhibition of 1889.[1] Was there no one who

[1] This is the text published in *Gil Blas* on 16th March 1903. That of the *Revue Blanche* of 15th November 1901 differs only by a few words and the insertion of these two sentences: 'In all this there is a painful straining after effect thanks to a text containing words written for the suburbs and situations which naturally make the music ridiculous. The action of the singers, the setting, so like a tin of sardines—one of the jealously guarded traditions of the Opera—bring the spectacle to an end and with it all hope for art.'

cared enough for Saint-Saëns to tell him that he had composed operas enough and that it would be better for him to cultivate his new-found hobby as an explorer? The contemplation of new skies might suggest to him more disinterested music. . . . Besides, it is obvious even to those who do not know him that he has no love for the public. His frantic desire to place the sea between him and his public on the occasion of each of his first performances is proof enough of that. He even apologizes, with an irony as charming as it is melancholy, for the concessions he believed himself obliged to make.'

The harshness of these scathing remarks is somewhat softened by Debussy, for he acknowledges his pitiless friend's petulant prejudice. Besides, when he had to write an account of the performance of 'Henry VIII' at the Opera, his article, though it did not lack irony, took a form and showed a spirit much more deferential: 'The revival of "Henry VIII" at the Opera merits our respectful greetings. We witness, perhaps, the passing of the last historical opera! . . . At least we hope so; and in any case it would be difficult to do better in that line than Meyerbeer. I do not mean to insinuate that M. Saint-Saëns did wrong in writing "Henry VIII". But he lacks that grandiloquent bad taste which characterizes the genius of Meyerbeer. He is more a musician than a dramatist, and only in the last extremity does he use the effects which this form of drama excuses. Then too, he brings to his task a sincerity unknown to the crafty Meyerbeer. And if Henry VIII does sing sugary cavatinas, you may be sure that M. Saint-

Saëns so wished and understood it. Besides, every one knows that the most bloodthirsty tiger can mew in a way that would touch the heart of a child. These over-sweet cavatinas are therefore scrupulously correct from the historical point of view, for the cruelty of Henry VIII was notorious. M. Camille Saint-Saëns has been accused of making concessions in his dramatic music: comparison with his symphonic music, in which he makes none, is inevitable; and the conclusion is drawn that this latter has not taken the direction that was expected of it. One forgets that M. Saint-Saëns is uncompromising in a contrary sense. . . . Whilst others are uncompromising in order to demolish everything, he is so only in order to preserve everything. His masters bequeathed to him formulas which he considers good, and the natural respect he holds them in prevents him from wishing to make any change in them. I do not think he should be blamed for this. I see in it evidence of an artistic clairvoyance which is rare enough in our days when many things change their name without achieving any other appreciable result. To be conscious of one's effort is undeniable proof of artistic honesty (La Fontaine has a fable on the subject).'

Massenet, the illustrious contemporary and rival of Saint-Saëns, usually receives much more sympathetic appreciation. He is one of those composers who have 'understood the true role of the art of music. . . . Music should humbly seek to please. . . .' Debussy always spoke of him with real friendliness. He admits, however, that this charming musician made the mistake of seeking too much after popular approval and of occasionally overstepping the limits of his domain in order to compose grand opera, 'straining his art for the sake of noisy effects'. Here is his first verdict: 'Massenet appears to have been the victim of the adulation of his lovely listeners whose fans fluttered so long to his glory. He wished above all to keep these perfumed wings fluttering around his name. Alas! one might as well attempt to train a troupe of butterflies. Perhaps it was only that he lacked patience and misunderstood the value of *silence*. . . . His influence on contemporary music is obvious, though some who owe him much fail to admit it; they meet the charge with hypocrisy . . . which is contemptible!'

Some months later Debussy devoted to Massenet a complete though brief essay under the title of 'D'Eve à Grisélidis'. It was his last contribution to the *Revue Blanche*. His intention was to trace 'not a portrait of M. Massenet, but something of the mental attitude he wished to express in the music he wrote'. He observes in the first place that 'music was never to M. Massenet *the universal voice* heard by Bach and Beethoven. Rather did he make of it a charming speciality. If one examines his already numerous works, it will be noticed that a constant thought directs their inevitable course. This it is which accounts for the reappearance in 'Grisélidis', his last opera, of some of the characteristics of 'Eve', one of his first works. Do we not see in this a sort of mysterious and compelling fate which explains M. Massenet's untiring quest in music for documents that will contribute to the history of the feminine soul. They are nearly all there, the faces of those women who formed the subjects of so many dreams! The smile of Manon in her pannier dress reappears on the lips of the modern Sappho to make men weep in the self-same way! The knife of the Navarraise is seen there, and the pistol of the unthinking Charlotte.'

Debussy makes a note here of some phrases that he republished and quoted exactly two years later as still expressing his opinion: 'We know too how this music throbs with emotional outbursts and never-ending embraces. The harmony is the encircling arm, the melody the curving neck. One bends over a woman's head, intent on discovering what goes on behind her brow. . . . Philosophers and healthy folk declare that nothing goes on there; but this does not altogether eliminate the opposite opinion, as M. Massenet's example proves, at least in melody. Moreover, it is to this care that he owes the place he occupies in contemporary art—a place which others secretly envy him and which, one may therefore assume, is not to be despised.'

Then Massenet is assigned his place in the history of contemporary opera: 'Fortune, being a woman, owed it to her sex to treat M. Massenet well and even to be unfaithful to him on occasions. She did not fail in this. Owing to his success, it was at one period considered good form to copy M. Massenet's melodic manias; then, suddenly, those who had so calmly pilfered his art treated him harshly. They reproached him with too great sympathy for

M. Mascagni and too little adoration for Wagner. The reproach is as unjust as it is inadmissible. M. Massenet was heroic enough to go on catering for his usual admirers amongst the ladies. And I must admit I fail to understand why it should be preferable to please old cosmopolitan "Wagnériennes" rather than perfumed young women, even though these latter may not play the piano very well. Once and for all he was quite right. . . . One reproach only can be levelled against him—his infidelity to Manon. . . . He had found there the setting that suited his flirtatious habits, and he should not have driven them into the Opera. At the Opera one does not flirt. Incomprehensible words are shouted aloud; and when vows are exchanged, it is with the approval of the trombones. Logically speaking, the fleeting tones of feeling must lose themselves amidst so much compulsory clamour. It would have been better had he continued to exercise his genius for clear tints and whispering melodies in works of airy lightness. They need not have ruled out experiments in art: they would have been more delicate, that is all. Surely plenty of musicians give us that forced style of music which suits the blaring of the trumpets. . . . Why swell their numbers needlessly and encourage a taste for the annoying music which we get from the neo-Wagnerians, and which really might do us the favour of returning to the land of its origin? With his unique gifts and his facile style, M. Massenet might have exerted considerable influence against this deplorable movement. It is not always good to howl with the wolves—a piece of advice which, it seems to me, the least intelligent of his lovely listeners might have given him.'

'These hasty notes' end with the remark that 'not every one can be a Shakespeare, but one may aim, without prejudice to oneself, at becoming a Marivaux'. The revival of 'Werther' at the Opéra-Comique in 1903 gave Debussy another opportunity for expressing his sympathy for Massenet. It is in this work that Massenet has best shown 'the charming quality of those gifts which make him the musical historian of the feminine soul'. The critic admires the feminine side of the score, especially the character of Sophie 'who is charming from one end of this piece to the other'. He deplores, however, that 'the dramatic side is exaggerated in the most annoying fashion'. He stresses 'the delightful indications of sentiment in the nocturnal return of Charlotte and Werther in the first act. Why must so much charm be suddenly transposed into howling trombones and rattling kettledrums? I can no more explain it than I can sufficiently deplore it. But M. Massenet is often guilty of tearing us from dreams, whose spell he had skilfully woven, by a noise which serves only to indicate to the public that it is time to applaud. I should like to assure him that the public would applaud without such a brutal invitation.'

The article, into which he inserts certain phrases already used in the *Revue Blanche*, ends on a note of great sympathy: 'M. Massenet may have realized that he would always be in the right, and that despite the jealousy of men, his lovely listeners of yore still retained the same passion for him. . . . Do they not in this music live again those moments when they were all the more beautiful for having been divinely moved? You may be sure such things are not forgotten. And the love of Massenet's music is a tradition that women will hand down from generation to generation for many a day to come. That should be glory enough for any man.'

When Debussy collected some of his articles to make up the volume of 'Monsieur Croche, anti-dilettante', he reproduced in the chapter on Massenet various extracts from the quotations just given, to which he added several very sympathetic paragraphs. He begins with this flattering appreciation of the influence on the great public of this delightful composer: 'Massenet was the most truly loved of contemporary musicians. Indeed, it is this love which placed him in the special position that he has occupied ever since in the musical world. His colleagues found it hard to forgive him this power of pleasing, which is indeed a real gift. This gift is not, however, indispensable, especially in art; and amongst other examples one may mention Johann Sebastian Bach, who never pleased in the sense in which the word is applied to Massenet. Would any one suggest that young dressmakers are in the habit of humming the "Matthew Passion"? I think not. But every one knows that they wake up in the morning singing "Manon" or "Werther". Let there be no mistake about it. There is a charm in such glory that will be secretly envied by more than one of the great purists who have but the laboured respect of the intellectuals to warm their hearts. He succeeded to the full in what he undertook to do, and in revenge for this it has been whispered that he was Paul Delmet's[1] best pupil, which pleasantry is in the worst possible taste. He has been much imitated, both outwardly and inwardly....'

On the subject of his popular colleague, Debussy adds these general reflections which were perhaps inspired as much by his own case as by that of Massenet: 'With some artists the first principle of wisdom is to endeavour to achieve the downfall of those they imitate. They call this contemptible manœuvre wrestling for art. There is something equivocal about this much-abused expression. It has, moreover, the defect of comparing art to a sport. In art it is more often than not with oneself alone that one must wrestle; and the victories one gains are all the greater. By a curious irony, however, one is apt to fear self-defeat, and so one prefers simply to be part of the public or else to follow one's friends, which comes to the same thing. In Napoleon's day all French mothers hoped that their sons would be Napoleons.... Many of these dreams have vanished in the tide of war. Besides, some destinies are unique. In its own way, Massenet's destiny is one of these.'

Other operas are performed side by side with the works of Gounod, Reyer, Saint-Saëns, Massenet. Of these Debussy does not care to remember any but 'Tamara', by Bourgault-Ducoudray. This neglected score, 'whose destinies, despite its mediocre success,

[1] Paul Delmet, Paris (1862-1904), composed songs which he sang himself in Montmartre cabarets frequented by artists. He was a pupil of Massenet (translator's note).

have probably not been accomplished', pleased Debussy because of the use of Oriental scales and the composer's contempt for harmonic conventions. But the National Academy of Music is also the National Academy of Dancing. While 'stupid ballets' are staged, a masterpiece, 'Namouna' by Lalo, has disappeared. 'Who knows what underhand enmity has buried it so deeply that it is never mentioned. . . . It is a pity, for music is the poorer. 'The wonderful ballet music' of 'Namouna' is heard only at concerts, 'thanks to an administration directed by M. Gailhard which is hostile to music, and which replaces it by musical importations reminiscent of the bazaar and the drinking booth.' When he was very young, Debussy was present at a performance of 'Namouna', and its memory remained very dear to him: 'I indulged in noisy but excusable enthusiasm. M. Vaucorbeil, a very gentle man who was then director of the Opera, had me summarily ejected. I bear him no grudge for that, but I recall this episode with feelings of deep emotion; and nothing has lessened the joyous and affectionate enthusiasm with which I still greet the name of Lalo.'

Debussy did not disdain the art of the ballet. During his visit to London in 1903 he went one night to the Empire Music Hall, 'as a reward for good behaviour during the "Ring" '. On seeing a ballet of Leopold de Wenzel danced he mused on 'what the atmosphere of the ballet ought to be. . . . The action should never be indicated except in that writing whose mysterious and charming symbols are found in the winged grace of the dancer's leg, which the rhythmic tension of her whole body renders in turn delicate as a flower and tender as a woman. The patter of the little feet, impatient or angry, can suggest love or hatred more clearly than the conventional gestures by means of which these sentiments are generally interpreted. . . . To this reality must be added the dreamy vagueness of a setting made up rather of changing lights than of definite lines. Let the music direct and supply the setting and by some spell prolong the silent fluttering of skirts of gauze in a like frou-frou of sounds. . . .'

Debussy sees in the entire repertory of the Opera 'no single effort that is really new. Nothing but the hum of a factory, constant repetition. One would think that when music enters the Opera it must don a uniform like a convict. It also assumes the pseudo-grandiose proportions of the edifice itself, taking its measure from the celebrated grand staircase which, owing to an error in perspective, or too much detail, really gives an ultimate impression of . . . meanness.'

Debussy could not remain indifferent to the need for change in a state of things so harmful to the destinies of the National art. Despite his contempt for this factory, characterized by 'industrious apathy', he proposed certain reforms. The Board of Directors 'to be composed of persons who would be too wealthy to bother about good business results but who, on the other hand, would take pride in having plenty of money to spend on the creation of beautiful things'; the selection of a 'Musical Director who would be entirely free and independent, whose duties would be to be well-informed in art and to guarantee beforehand a programme of retrospective and carefully chosen works'; the extension and improvement of the repertoire and the artistic personnel; finally—this last clause in a project of lyric reform is vague enough—'above all to give a great deal of music and not deliberately keep the public in an attitude of indifference.'

If our critic's dictum is to be taken into account, the choice of the French repertory would not be easy. Debussy, in his reference to retrospective and delicately chosen works, evidently has in mind Rameau, and perhaps Mozart; Gluck also, but only in order to reject this composer's ultra-German works. Among the elect would be Weber, of whom no critic ever wrote with greater sympathy and admiration. He would reject all the so-called French opera of 1830 and 1840. Was it not, in the words of Rossini, 'le sabbat des Juifs'? Of the nineteenth-century composers Gounod and Massenet are practically the only ones to find favour. With regard to new works, what could have been found in 1903 by a director 'well informed in art'? He would have been obliged to set aside practically the entire repertory chosen at this period by Pedro Gailhard at the Opera and by Albert Carré at the Opéra-Comique, including certainly Georges Hüe's long work the 'Roi de Paris', and probably the 'Ouragan' of Alfred Bruneau.

The 'Roi de Paris' is, in spite of the talent of its composer, 'just one more opera to add to the rest'. After the first performance in 1901, Debussy disposes of it in a few lines: 'The subject is historical since it deals with the assassination of the Duc de Guise.

To begin with, this is not one of the noblest things in the history of France, and there was no necessity to remind us of it with the added aggravation of music. Besides, people dressed very badly in those days: the men appeared to wear inelegant life-belts, and the women wore their waists where one least expected to find them. If opera is to be transformed into a series of historical lectures, why not endeavour to find episodes less impaired by political and ludicrous intrigue? (I should like to suggest the period of Louis Philippe, an unexplored but fertile field. . . .) M. Georges Hüe has put too much music to this story; it prevents one from hearing the words of the poem which appear to have been inspired by those great and unforgettable twin spirits—Bouvard and Pécuchet.[1] It would be most unseemly to blame M. Georges Hüe for not achieving a masterpiece; and the fact that the rather dubious character of Henry III was assigned to a tenor shows a delicate sense of historic interpretation.'

Debussy admitted the great merit of the composer of the 'Roi de Paris' in his long account of 'Titania', an opera whose fairy theme gave him an opportunity of recalling 'Oberon' and Weber: 'M. Georges Hüe is acquainted with all the formulas the sum total of which goes to produce a really able musician. He manipulates the component parts of the orchestra with a skilful hand. . . .' He has a 'very true feeling for what is melancholy and even tragic in everyday things and people. . . .' He may become 'eventually the admirable musician—exponent of sorrow—

[1] Characters in a novel by Flaubert (translator's note).

which everything in his work leads me to hope for. . . .' Where he went wrong, in Debussy's eyes, was undoubtedly in his choice of librettos.

Alfred Bruneau's lyrical drama, 'L'Ouragan', is treated by the critic with considerably more respect than was the 'Roi de Paris'. It aroused at once friendliness and anxiety in Debussy. Friendliness for the personal qualities of his music, the freedom of his grammar, the overpowering force of the movement and anxiety because of his symbolistic and Wagnerian tendencies. The Wagnerism is looked upon as nullifying any virtue in the work!

Alfred Bruneau 'has, more than any other musician, a delightful contempt for formulas. He makes his way through harmonies without worrying about their correctness; he perceives melodic associations that some hastily qualify as monstrous, when they are simply unusual. The third act of this drama appears to me the most definitely successful. The music is wild, intense, and far more telling than the facile tragedy of the plot. The latter should be more rapid and not linger over psychological discussions on the comparative value of the jealousy experienced by two characters in this act. Besides, the music roughly jostles the words and seems to say: 'Get out of my way. Can't you see I am the stronger? And this settles everything. . . .'

When a concert performance was given of 'Penthésilée', a symphonic poem with voice, of which the verses were by Catulle Mendès and the score by Alfred Bruneau, Debussy had already called attention to the supremacy accorded to the music: 'It is always the vexed question whether music is to be the master or the slave. I am glad to say that in 'Penthésilée', Bruneau has chosen the latter form. How right he was is shown in those orchestral passages, so rich in musical qualities that adorn with passion the colourless verses of Catulle Mendès. . . .' In this poem, 'which is a great credit to French music', Alfred Bruneau shows his 'gifts of realism in declamation as well as in orchestral setting', and Debussy rejoices to see him 'less taken up with *naturalism* than he is in his lyrical dramas'. He then comments on the valuable qualities of these theatrical works as well as on their chief defect, which, in his eyes, is the realism of the librettos.

In the expression of his opinion on Alfred Bruneau his sympathy is apparent: '. . . I know to what heights he attains through this zeal (for naturalism) and how estimable is his artistic courage which prompted him to sacrifice to it the ardour of his musical imagination. It is with some embarrassment that I confess my admiration for this poem and my opinion that he is more at ease in it than in the dramas written for him by Émile Zola. I admit that these dramas contain passages of profound and original beauty such as the third act of "Ouragan", where the music attains to the heights of ancient tragedy in expressing all the horror felt by the characters and by that other character—the sea—towering and thundering! Certain pages of "Le Rêve" too, so full of tenderness, and many other things which I remember but cannot definitely name at the moment. Still, it seems to me that if music is not made for the purpose of specializing in elusive dreams, neither does it gain anything by being hemmed in by the everyday things of life. It is strained in recording cries that are too human, for its very essence is founded on mystery. . . .'

In his account of 'L'Ouragan' Debussy makes certain reservations regarding one of the characters and the symbol he represents. This judgement of Zola's poem, 'more fertile in situations than in strictly lyrical words', is preceded by the following lines: 'I appear to make restrictions and yet it is difficult to do so in dealing with this work. One must take it or leave it. One must love its faults as well as its good points: otherwise, I repeat, it is impossible. At any rate it is the work of a man who seeks truth through suffering. That is not common in our days when so many so-called masters seek only to reach the hundredth performance through a tradition of lies bequeathed by one greater than them all.'

The identity of this false benefactor 'greater than them all' is easily guessed at. It is Wagner.[1] This reference serves as a pretext to start a discussion on dramatic music and to generalize upon it. 'L'affaire Wagner' obtrudes itself. Debussy deals with it in a few lines: 'Wagner has left us various formulas for adapting music to the theatre, the futility of which will be seen one day. That he should, for special reasons, have established the "leit-motiv-guide" for the use of those who cannot follow a score, is all very well, and simplified matters for him. . . . What is more serious is that he has accus-

[1] See Chapter VII of this volume, dealing with Debussy's criticisms of the works of Wagner.

tomed us to make the music servilely dependent on the characters. I shall try to make myself clear regarding this matter, in my opinion the chief cause of the confusion which exists in the dramatic music of our times: Music has a rhythm whose secret force directs the development. The emotions of the soul have another, which is more instinctively general and is influenced by numerous events. The juxtaposition of these two rhythms creates perpetual conflict. They are not simultaneous. Either the music gets out of breath in running after a character, or else the character sits down on a note to allow the music to catch up with him. Amazing encounters between these two forces sometimes take place, and Wagner can claim the honour of having provoked some of them. But that is due to chance which more often than not proves clumsy or disappointing in its results. So, when all is said and done, the application of the symphonic form to dramatic action might end by killing dramatic music, instead of serving it as was triumphantly proclaimed in the days when Wagner reigned undisputed over lyrical drama.'

Following on this general theory is a simple opinion on the main theme: 'The drama of MM. Zola and Bruneau boasts of many symbols, and I must confess I do not understand the necessity for this exaggerated use of symbols. Some people appear to lose sight of the fact that the finest of all symbols is music. Naturally, the symbol calls for the "leit-motiv"; and here again we have music once more overburdened with little persistent phrases that insist on making themselves heard in spite of everything. To sum up, the pretence that such a succession of chords will represent such a feeling, and such a phrase such a character, is merely an ill-chosen game of anthropometry. Is there no other way? I address the question to M. Bruneau, whose imaginative will appears to me suited to the finding of admirable solutions. . . .'

French musicians should not have followed this 'tradition of lies'. They should never have strayed from home: 'Wagner is essential to the efflorescence of art in Germany—an amazing efflorescence, but one which is at the same time virtually a burial. One may doubt, without prejudice, that he ever had anything to do in France, as far as influencing our mode of thought is concerned. It is doubtless true that the future alone can judge events impartially, but we may at least be allowed to state the brutal fact that there is no longer any French tradition.'

Since the dramatic revolutions fomented by two foreigners—Gluck and Wagner—the French theatre is trying to find its way. Modern lyrical drama is 'a Glucko-Wagnerian importation, quite foreign to our genius'. Towards the end of 1916, when writing of Emmanuel Chabrier, Debussy still deplored this taste which persisted among our musicians; and nothing seemed to him more pathetic than 'this neo-Wagnerian school in which French genius foundered amidst counterfeit Wotans wearing high boots and Tristans in velvet tunics'.

Not even the efforts and talent of Vincent d'Indy succeeded in establishing perfectly balanced models.

'Fervaal' is still subject to the Wagnerian tradition, although d'Indy is protected against it 'by his conscience and his contempt for the grandiloquent hysteria of the Wagnerian heroes'. In spite of current opinion, 'Wagner never had a really deep influence on d'Indy's work; for the heroic antics of the one could have nothing in common with the artistic probity of the other'. As to 'L'Étranger', although this work has serious defects, Debussy holds it in great esteem: 'L'Étranger' is what dogmatic people call a dignified and pure manifestation of art. In my humble opinion it is more than that. It gives free rein to formulas that are certainly pure and dignified, but which likewise possess the cold, blue, fine hardness of steel. The music produced was so beautiful, though restrained, its mastery so amazing, that one hardly dared to feel emotion—it would not have been proper.'

The idea of the renovation of the art of d'Indy was again referred to by Debussy in an account of the prelude to 'L'Étranger': 'Vincent d'Indy's pure musical drama'. This work seemed to him to inaugurate a new era in the French master's 'very honest art': 'There one is at ease, free from the duty which d'Indy formerly imposed on his friends of admiring the fine mastery of his compositions, even though this was detrimental to his ideas. . . . On the other hand, logically, he was bound to attain to this truth: that composition, no matter how admirable, has never been able to replace emotion; that the craft can achieve the expression of beauty only by suppressing all use of abstract combinations.'

In his account of the first performance of 'L'Étranger', Debussy observes that doubtless 'Vincent d'Indy will be reproached with having freed himself, and no longer caring so much for the game of the "Rendez-vous des thèmes", which was the joy of old Wagnerians who were specially notified in advance'. Far from reproaching him with this, his colleague regrets that he should not have 'freed himself entirely from this passion for explaining and emphasizing everything, which mars some of the finest scenes in "L'Étranger".'

Debussy's narrative continues. There is a careful analysis of the drama and the characters; special commendation for the simple line of two phrases that express the character of the stranger: 'Modern music has never expressed itself with deeper piety or more Christian charity. It is in truth a profound conviction in d'Indy which renders these two phrases so superlatively good. They throw more light on the inner meaning of the drama than could any symphonic comment.' Lastly, in general appreciation, he says: 'Let him who will seek fathomless symbols in this action. I like to perceive in it a humanity which Vincent d'Indy has clothed with symbols only in order to render more unbridgeable that eternal divorce between beauty and the vulgarity of the masses. I will not dwell on questions of technique. I wish rather to pay a tribute to the serene goodness which hovers over this work, to the effort of will which sought to avoid all complication, and above all, to the quiet courage of Vincent d'Indy in surpassing himself. And if a while ago I complained of too much music, it is because here and there it seems to me to interfere with the perfect efflorescence which adorns so many pages of "L'Étranger" with unforgettable beauty. In a word, this work is an admirable lesson for those who pin their faith to the odious imported fashion for aesthetics, which crushes music beneath the wheels of realism.'

There is too much music, an excess of beautiful music, in this fine work. The scene calls for quicker action. Certainly Debussy does not approve of symphonic treatment in theatrical work. The public is in a hurry. It follows the drama, and has not time for the complications of the purely musical development. This fact was stated in connexion with another piece, of similar name, 'L'Étrangère', by Max d'Ollone: 'One must certainly admit that the dramatic symphony will soon be as dead as a doornail. . . .'

The study of so many efforts leads Debussy to conclude that 'to sum up, we have perhaps not yet found the lyrical form corresponding to our present attitude of mind. The fundamental error lies in not realizing that Wagner's genius marked the close of a period and not a path leading to the Future! The idea of compelling the symphonic development to depend on the dramatic action was but a device, which never proved of much service except to Wagner and German thought. In adopting it our passion for clarity could only be weakened and indeed stifled. That is why we mark time without rightly knowing where we are going. However, there are several roads on which we could find once more the tracks of French thought from which we have strayed.'

Which are these roads? There is no mistaking the forbidden ones,—historical opera, the lyrical drama inspired by Wagner. . . . Is comic opera with its modern derivatives more acceptable? The creation of 'Muguette', set to music by Edmond Missa, a comrade of his youth, provided Debussy with a double opportunity for stating his theory on the subject. On the day following the first performance, in a short article, he admits that this work is very out of date, reminiscent of 'periods one believed to be buried for ever in a drawer beneath old lace. It is quite touching—in the same way as would be the discovery of a daguerreotype portrait of one's grandmother. . . .' A few days later he returned to the subject in a feuilleton—this time to generalize. The fault he finds in this work 'is that it clings to forms that are bad because they are not original and never have been'. This fault is not peculiar to the author of 'Muguette': 'Truth to tell, the others are more astute and flavour the old ideas, as does the world, with a modern sauce. With a little luck and a lot of stirring, it passes muster and one is acclaimed a master by general consent.'

This 'modern sauce' is quite evidently that used by the twentieth-century Italians to season their realistic operas. This transalpine realism worried Debussy not a little, especially on account of its possible influence on French music. Puccini, Leoncavallo, Mascagni, owe to this nationalist reaction on the part of Debussy the merciless treatment they received at his hands. They are tied to the aesthetics of Verdi, that of his early works such as 'Traviata', in which we already find the 'formulas that have become dear to the young Italian school: the "entr'acte" imperturbably encored, the romance that brings out the handkerchiefs, &c. . . .' Nevertheless, the sincere inspiration of this old work is more sympathetic than that of the realists: 'One travels from ballad to ballad, deriving pleasure from any true passion one may find here and there. There is never any pretence at depth. It is all on the surface, and in spite of the sadness of the situations, the sun is always shining. Aesthetically, this art is certainly false, for life cannot be interpreted in songs. But Verdi has a way of giving the lie to life in a heroic fashion which is perhaps finer than the effort at reality attempted by the young Italian school.'

The worst crime of Puccini and Leoncavallo lies in their having taken a French novel, the 'Vie de Bohême', as the theme of operas that are radically Italian; and in spite of their pretence at character-study, of having achieved nothing more than simple anecdote. Mascagni treats his audience 'to sundry bits of gossip aggravated by declamation which fails to depict life and merely shows cleverness. It is fatiguing to the last degree!' The works of these three musicians are based on what Debussy in 1913 called 'the veristic film formula, by which the characters fling themselves on one another and tear the melodies from one another's lips; in which a whole life is depicted in one act, including birth, marriage and assassination. . . . The minimum of music is required, for the simple reason that there is not time for much.' Debussy repeats in varying but always equally bitter terms the fact that he could not condone 'this odious imported fashion for aesthetics which crushes music beneath the wheels of realism'.

It should be stated that this inferior art had its effect on certain French composers and this influence is reciprocal. The verists are false disciples of Massenet, that very individual master who cannot altogether escape the influence of the surprising action of his own pupils. The works of the latter may be looked upon as 'skilful counterfeits of French music, unless the contrary is the case'.

Debussy was at times pessimistic concerning the future of stage music in France. Replying to an inquiry on the orientation of music in 1902, he said: 'As to contemporary dramatic music, it moved from Wagnerian metaphysics to Italian tit-bits of gossip—which hardly suggests a very French orientation. Perhaps it will eventually achieve that clarity and conciseness of expression which are the fundamental qualities of French genius. Will there be a return of that versatile fancy of which this art alone is capable, and which appears to have been lost sight of in experiments which, obviously, must soon banish all music?' At other times he showed greater confidence: 'We have good fighting material. There are men and works that furnish a telling answer to these petty questions by the fine intellectual activity which is found only in France. This must be made clear. So many efforts to rescue music from the paths of falsehood by restoring her original beauty cannot be stifled by Realism—that workshop of nothingness.'

Debussy himself, when engaged on the slow elaboration of 'Pelléas et Mélisande', had struggled arduously to avoid being dragged into the ruts of dramatic falsehood. He tells about it in a statement which he handed to the general secretary of the Opéra-Comique on the occasion of a revival of the work. The statement, which is of deep historic and artistic interest, contained the following principal passages:

'For a long time (before 1893, during which year he had read Maeterlinck's drama) I sought to compose music for the theatre. But the form I wished to employ was so unusual that after various efforts I had almost abandoned the idea. Previous research in pure music had led me to hate classical development, whose beauty is merely technical and of interest only to the highbrows of our class. I desired for music that freedom of which she is capable perhaps to a greater degree than any other art, as she is not confined to an exact reproduction of nature, but only to the mysterious affinity between Nature and the Imagination.

'After several years of passionate pilgrimage to Bayreuth, I began to entertain doubts as to the Wagnerian formula; or rather, it seemed to me that it could serve only the particular case of Wagner's genius. He was a great collector of formulas. He assembled them all into one, which appears individual to those who are ill acquainted with music. And without denying his genius one may say that he placed a period to the music of his time in much the same way as Victor Hugo did for poetry. The thing, then, was to find what came *after Wagner's time* but not *after Wagner's manner.*

'The drama of "Pelléas", which, in spite of its fantastic atmosphere, contains much more humanity than the so-called *documents on life*, appeared to me to be admirably suited to my purpose. The sensitiveness of the suggestive language could be carried into the music and orchestral setting. I have also tried to obey a law of beauty which appears to be singularly ignored in dealing with dramatic music. The characters of this drama endeavour to sing like real persons, and not in an arbitrary language built on antiquated traditions. Hence the reproach levelled at my alleged partiality for monotone declamation, in which there is no trace of melody. . . . To begin with, this is untrue. Besides, the feelings of a character cannot be continually expressed in melody. Then too, dramatic melody should be totally different from melody in general. . . . The people who go to listen to music at the theatre are, when all is said and done, very like those one sees gathered around a street-singer! There, for a penny, one may indulge in melodic emotions. . . . One even notices greater patience than is practised by many subscribers to our state-endowed theatres and even *a wish to understand* which, one might even go so far as to say, is totally lacking in the latter public.

'By a singular irony, this public, which cries out for something new, is the very one that shows alarm and scoffs whenever one tries to wean it from old habits and the customary humdrum noises. . . . This may seem incomprehensible; but one must not forget that a work of art or an effort to produce beauty are always regarded by some people as a personal affront.

'I do not pretend to have discovered everything in "Pelléas"; but I have tried to trace a path that others may follow, broadening it with individual discoveries which will, perhaps, free dramatic music from the heavy yoke under which it has existed for so long.'

The uncertainty and confusion caused by the problem of opera urged Debussy towards scenic music or melodrama in which he achieved a masterpiece in the 'Martyre de Saint Sébastien'. In this connexion too, he has clearly stated his principles: 'I wrote my music as though I had been asked to write it for a church. The result is decorative music, if you like, a noble text interpreted in sounds and rhythms; and when in the last act the saint ascends into Heaven I believe I realized all that I have felt and experienced in the thought of the Ascension. Did I succeed? It no longer matters to me. In our times we have not in our souls the faith of other days. Is the faith expressed by my music orthodox or not? I cannot say. It is my faith, mine, singing in all sincerity. If it interests you to know it, I may as well tell you that I wrote in two months a score which in the ordinary way would have taken me a year, and that I put into practice, if I may say so, my theories on scenic music which, to my mind, should be something more than the vague buzzing that too often accompanies verse or prose, and should be closely incorporated with the text. . . .'

Besides, Debussy had retained anxious memories of the theatrical experiment made at the Opéra-Comique in 1902 when 'Pelléas et Mélisande' was under rehearsal. He confessed his past anxiety in January 1908 when writing for *Musica* an appreciation of his leading lady, Mary Garden: 'The scenic realization of a work of art, no matter how beautiful, is always contrary to the inner vision which drew it in turns from its alternatives of doubt and enthusiasm. Think of the charming lie in which your characters and you yourself dwelt for so long, when it sometimes seemed they were about to rise, tangible, from the silent pages of the manuscript. Is it any wonder if one is bewildered on seeing them come to life before one's eyes through the intervention of such and such an artist? It is almost fear that is experienced; and one hardly dares to speak to them. In truth, they are like phantoms. From this moment, nothing remains of the old dream. The mind of another interposes between you and it. The setting materializes under the deft movements of scene-shifters and the birds of the forest find their nests in the orchestral wood-wind. The lights are turned on. The play of the curtain curtails or prolongs emotion. Applause,—aggressive noises resembling the sounds of a distant fête where you are but the parasite of a glory which does not always prove to be what you desired. For, to succeed in the theatre most often implies a response to anonymous desires and assimilable emotion. . . .'

Debussy's ideal was too high and too pure not to be lowered and soiled by contact with the theatre. Fear, perhaps even disgust, is revealed in the above recollections of the production, infinitely delicate and beautiful though it was, of 'Pelléas et Mélisande'. These painful feelings of a pure musician face to face with realization stark and insincere help to explain the persistent satire inspired in the critic-composer by the performance of any kind of music-drama: to him they were unfortunate attempts at an impossible reconciliation of the opposing interests of the theatre and the symphony. When one has read through the various counts in the indictment which Debussy brought against his colleagues, young and old, one realizes that his quarrel with them was as much in the interests of drama as of music. One then understands that the author of 'Pelléas et Mélisande', one of whose Rameau-like qualities was 'that pliable subtlety in voicing the syllables of our gentle tongue', after having written an inimitable score to a very fine poem, could not definitely devote his genius to the production of another work on the lines of Opera.

VII
The Works of Wagner

IN common with so many of his contemporaries, Claude Debussy had been, in his young days, an enthusiastic admirer of Wagner. Having won the Prix de Rome, he spent long months at the Villa Medici, where he put in some of his time playing over and over again the score of 'Tristan and Isolde'. For some years he made 'passionate pilgrimages to Bayreuth'. Then he began 'to harbour doubts concerning the Wagnerian formula', and to think 'that it could only serve the particular case of Wagner's genius'. Little by little the Germanic influence waned, until he abjured his old faith and began to profess persistent anti-Wagnerism. The building up of this new creed, which was instinctive in a young French composer regaining consciousness of the national tradition, may have been occasioned in the first place by the study of Russian music and particularly by the revelation of Mussorgsky's works.

His abjuration did not cause him to forget his old love, whose riotous strength he frequently admitted in his articles. On April 6th, 1903, he recalled in *Gil Blas* the representations of 'Parsifal' at Bayreuth in 1889: '1889! Delightful period when I was madly Wagnerian. Why am I no longer so? . . .' On June 10th, narrating his Prix de Rome impressions in the same paper, he proclaims in the following piquant terms the reality of his vanished Wagnerism: 'At that period, when I was Wagnerian to the point of forgetting the simplest principles of civility. . . .' Again one divines the vanished power of this Wagnerism when, in 1903, Debussy, listening to the works of Siegfried, the great man's heir, excuses the son for not having escaped 'the bewitching atmosphere of Bayreuth' and having 'essayed to drink the lees of the old magician's cup'.

Debussy flung his idol to the ground, but he did not on that account dream of denying the musical genius of Wagner. One glimpses here and there in his writings the fact that he never ceased to cherish a real affection for 'Tristan and Isolde', a score in which 'Chopin's charming soul is reflected here and there in the music, directing its passion'. He did not shut his ears to the 'ardent beauty' of the 'Ring'. This fourfold work, to which he devotes an article of peevish censure, contains, so he admits, 'things of unforgettable beauty which silence all criticism. . . . It is irresistible as the sea. . . .' But what made the works of Wagner hateful in the eyes of Debussy was their very Wagnerism—that is to say, their dramatic system and musical procedure; also their influence, which he considered fatal to French music. In the preceding chapter we have seen the species of horror which Richard Wagner's dramatic and musical manner inspired in Debussy, as well as the excessive reaction provoked in a French artist by the diffusion of profoundly German aesthetics. There is nothing further to note here beyond detailed criticisms of the works of the German Master.

As these critiques of Wagner were misunderstood by uncompromising Wagnerians, Debussy was often obliged to explain his censure of this disproportionate art, the imitation of which is opposed to the French temperament. In 1909, replying to a journalist, he stated, as already cited, that since his Prix de Rome days he had not ceased in his efforts to forget what he had been taught; to become French once more, and to rid himself of ponderous Germanic influences. Of these influences, Wagner is the most overwhelming and long-winded: 'Wagner's genius is certainly unquestionable. Wagner has above all created an art which is individual to him, and those who came under his influence have taken only its form. It is his drama above all that is false from our French point of view. The idea of spreading one drama over four evenings! Is this admissible, especially when in these four evenings you always hear the same thing? The characters and the orchestra pass on the same themes in turn to one another, and then comes the "Twilight of the Gods", which is again a résumé of what you have already heard. I repeat that all this is inadmissible for those who love clarity and conciseness.'

Further details of Debussy's point of view (or rather, point of hearing) with regard to Wagner are found in the few lines of witty controversy which he published in *Gil Blas* when he first became a contributor to that paper. A fellow composer and critic of his, Victorien Joncières, who was an ardent Wagnerian, had stated in the *Petit Bleu*, so Debussy says, 'that I made Wagner out to be a "raseur" and himself "vieille barbe". . . . To begin with, this is incorrect. Also, it is not in accordance with the courtesy I invariably show to the aged. M. Joncières will do me the honour of believing that it would be impossible for me to apply to Wagner an epithet so justly applicable to those who imitated him too closely.'

It would appear, however, that Debussy would have been quite capable of applying to Wagner, as to his most faithful imitators, the epithet which, he declares, he did not use. This probability strikes one on reading through some of the articles he published in the *Revue Blanche* and *Gil Blas* in 1901 and 1903. Wagner is seldom treated with respect; on the contrary, disrespect breaks out in every line.

In his very first article in the *Revue Blanche* he shot two or three darts. Chevillard had conducted a few pages of the 'Ring'. These fragmentary performances appeared to him to show 'refined taste and perfect tact'. This appreciation was in answer to those fierce and insatiable Wagnerians who will not be satisfied with simple examples taken from colossal scores: 'People who put on learned airs when speaking of the "Ring" would, perhaps, hesitate to sit out a complete performance of that musical "Bottin".[1] Besides, M. Chevillard possesses an orchestral gift which lends singular animation to the tin-plate and skins in which the characters in "Siegfried" are attired; and they appear more human when the imagination supplies what is lacking in the actual, inadequately legendary, setting.'

[1] The French equivalent of Kelly's Directory.

The critic's second article opens with a statement whose free and easy humour emphasizes his anti-Wagnerian tendency: 'On the last Sunday of March (Palm Sunday), the Sunday Concerts rang changes on Wagner, but without result. At Monsieur Colonne's the menu was varied; at Monsieur Chevillard's there was but one course, but that was tetralogical. Heaven avenged itself by pouring on the unfortunate dilettanti all its reserves of rain. Is He who reigns in the heavens a Wagnerian, or is He not, as somebody (you know who, don't you?) said?' Any pretext is good enough for bitter words, for heaping satirical censure on the German master. Now it is a reference to 'some highly-flavoured masterpieces of Richard Wagner: Tannhäuser, Siegmund, Lohengrin, trumpeted once more the claims of the leit-motiv . . . pompous palaver in high helmets and without definite warrant'. Again, he picks out certain famous passages from 'Tannhäuser' for ruthless condemnation: the air in the musical contest, whose tediousness is emphasized by 'the noble and unctuous eloquence of the gentle Wolfram'; the other air with which the principal character answers, which he describes as 'a kind of military allegro'; the song, 'Oh, Star of Eve', also sung by Wolfram, the 'incorrigible' . . . . Even his praise of the beautiful finale of the 'Walküre' is not untinged with irony. The critic scoffs at the incantation of the fire, whose 'pyrotechnic effects cannot fail to delight any public'.

The leit-motiv system exasperates Debussy and calls forth more than one witty remark. Having just heard at the English Opera at Covent Garden the entire 'musical Bottin' of the 'Ring of the Nibelungs', he gave free rein to his ill humour in *Gil Blas* on June 1st, 1903: 'It is hard to imagine the state to which the strongest brain is reduced by listening for four nights to the "Ring". A leit-motiv quadrille is danced, in which Siegfried's horn executes a strange vis-à-vis figure with the theme of Wotan's spear, whilst the curse motiv performs the most maddening "gentlemen's chain". It is worse than obsession. It is possession. You no longer belong to yourself. You are but a leit-motiv moving in an atmosphere of tetralogy. No ingrained habit of courtesy will in future prevent us from hailing our fellow-beings by the cries of the Walkyrie: Hoyotoho!... Heiah!... Hoyohei!... Isn't it gay! Hoyohei! What will the newsboys say! Heiaho! Ah, my lord! How unbearable these people in skins and helmets become by the fourth night!... Remember they never appear without the accompaniment of their accursed leit-motiv. Some of them even sing it! Which suggests a harmless lunatic who, on presenting his visiting-card, would declaim his name in song...'

These indicatory motives oblige the music to 'burden itself with little persistent phrases that insist on being heard in spite of everything. The pretence that a certain series of chords represents such a feeling and a certain phrase such a character, is an unexpected game of anthropometry.'

Debussy would reluctantly admit that Wagner 'had created the *leit-motiv guide* for the use of those who cannot find their way in a score. It is splendid and allows one to get on quicker.' He would tolerate the childish game of anthropometry whilst wishing that the musicians would reject the signposts, if this procedure in thematic composition did not involve the strict subjection to the drama of music 'rendered servilely dependent on the characters'.

We have seen, in connexion with Alfred Bruneau's 'Ouragan', the critic's clear assertions attributing to this servility the disturbance in dramatic music in his day. Debussy admitted that this servility, so usual in Wagner's scores, had been lessened in the German master's last work. 'Parsifal' is, in his eyes, 'an admirable proof of the futility of formulas—a magnificent contradiction of the "Ring"'. This theory, which was launched in answer to a query on German influence, was thus explained and elucidated: 'In "Parsifal", the last effort of a genius before whom one must perforce bow, Wagner tried to be less authoritative towards music; it breathes with greater ease. There is no longer the nervous breathlessness entailed by the pursuit of the sickly passion of a Tristan; the infuriated cries of an Isolde; or the grandiloquent commentary of an inhuman Wotan. In all Wagner's music nothing attains to more serene beauty than the prelude to the third act of "Parsifal" and the entire Good Friday episode. . . .' The decorative side of the sacred work Debussy describes as 'of supreme beauty. There are orchestral sonorities that are unique and unexpected, noble and strong. It is one of the finest monuments of sound ever erected to the indestructible glory of music.'

In his various articles on Wagnerian operas Debussy is loud in praise of the music, but his enthusiasm suddenly flags when he turns to the drama. At once he embarks on a scathing satire of this literature, interspersed with fresh praises of the music. Incessant contradiction throws him from blame to praise, from enthusiastic appreciation to violent censure. These dramatic diatribes, as well as the alternative praise of the music, deserve to be quoted, at least in part.

Here is a long critique of the libretto of the 'Ring of the Nibelungs' which in the course of four evenings offers 'innumerable commentaries on this story of a ring that is lost and found again, passing from hand to hand as in the game of Find the Ring'. At every page the piece emphasizes 'Wotan's lack of understanding of all that goes on around him. For this chief of the Gods is certainly the most stupid of them.... He spends his time listening indefatigably to a story which the most insignificant of the dwarfs languishing in the workshops of the Nibelungs would understand. But all he can do is brandish his spear or cause flames to burst out, or commit irreparable blunders that place everything in jeopardy. But you will say that four evenings have to be filled.... A titanic undertaking, so hardened Wagnerians declare! The superhuman effort of a proud conceit that must have both quality and quantity.... An effort unfortunately spoiled by the German mania for hammering persistently on the intellectual nail, for fear of not being understood. In this way it becomes tedious through idle repetition.

'The characters in the "Ring" follow one another in a sea of boundless pride.... They never trouble to justify their actions. They enter, exit, kill one another with absolute disregard for probability. . . . Thus, in the "Twilight of the Gods", Hagen does away with Siegfried to avenge that horrible dwarf his father; and not one of the skin-clad witnesses of this cowardly act discovers the means of destroying him in his turn . . . though, goodness knows, they are unmitigated ruffians. In this same drama, Brünnhild, the strong virgin, allows Hagen and Gunther to humbug her like an innocent little First Communicant. It is really not worth while being a daughter of the gods! Then, too, she loves Siegfried, the military hero, so proud of his fine cuirass. He is in some degree her brother (owing to Wotan's misconduct, all the characters in the "Ring" are more or less brothers and sisters). Was it necessary for her to be avenged and to betray him with such a lack of greatness; and does the fact that she has lost her divine nature excuse her attitude, which suggests a nursemaid deceived? . . . A few minutes later—Siegfried having been done away with—a godlike inconsistency allows her to appear and declare that she alone was worthy to hover around his body and to perform the necessary rites. The poor skin-clad creatures aforementioned have never understood the high-minded attitude of this young hero, who lacked only a little worldly wisdom, his time being entirely taken up in killing dragons, listening to the song of birds, &c. As if there could be any doubt as to her responsibility for this death and its regrettable consequences. . . . Hoyotoho! Bravo . . . Hoyohei! Serves her right!

'As I have already remarked, parts of the "Ring" are childish fairy tales. And if on the one hand it is not at all ridiculous to have dragons singing and birds giving invaluable advice; a bear, a horse, two crows and two black sheep (I forget the rest) charmingly introduced, on the other hand this mixture of wild humanity and godlike inhumanity does not blend satisfactorily! It would perhaps have been better to have had the courage to plunge up to the neck into improbability without bothering about human weakness, which could only mar the splendour of the Tetralogical heroes. . . . Sapristi! be gods, if you will . . . be fairies, but do not give lessons in humanity that are as unprofitable as they are conventional. . . .'

Having reached this point, Debussy realizes that he is indulging in dramatic criticism and that he has strayed from his domain. So he promptly proclaims his not altogether whole-hearted admiration of the four scores: 'Let me rather assure you that there is ardent beauty in the "Tetralogy". . . . In moments of tedium, when one really does not know whether to blame the music or the drama, passages of unforgettable beauty suddenly appear and silence all criticism. . . . It is irresistible as the sea. Sometimes it lasts but a moment, often longer. . . . I won't insult you by pointing out these beauties; possibly they might not be quite to your taste. Though indeed, there are enough to satisfy every appetite.'

What conclusion does he reach on the subject of this overwhelming and sublime work? Something very unexpected after such biting satire: 'One does not criticize a work of such magnitude as the "Ring". . . .' And Debussy indulges in a lengthy sentence whose pomposity, worthy of its German subject, must surely have made him smile: 'I don't quite like that last phrase,' he admits after writing it, 'but it is admirable as applied to Wagner.' Here are the pompous lines: 'It is a monument whose architectural lines are merged in the Infinite. Its too sumptuous greatness renders futile the legitimate desire to grasp its proportions. In spite of oneself one feels that the displacement of the tiniest stone in the edifice might bring it crashing to the ground after the manner of the final catastrophe which concludes the "Twilight of the Gods", where all humanity is swallowed up whilst the gods on Olympus smile imperturbably at the vain efforts of the modern Prometheus.'

He wrote similar pleasantries on Wagnerian dramatic art when the Concerts Lamoureux gave 'Rhinegold' after the Italian manner: 'It is two hours of music with the ancient gods, the aquatic flirtation of the Daughters of the Rhine with the dwarf Alberich. It is the absorbing story of the theft of the Ring, in which Wotan, leader of the gods, behaves just like some hero of Ponson du Terrail who might have read the "Arabian Nights". And it flames . . . it burns . . . it thunders. There are giants two and a half metres high and dwarfs half a metre (as is customary). Then, it concludes with a staircase made of an obliging rainbow (which is obviously nicer than a lift, but more expensive) by means of which the gods go home. In a word, it is modern fairy lore with all its appurtenances. Not even the merry character so essential to the fairy tale is wanting. Here it is represented by the crafty and tale-bearing Loge, the same who later on (in the Walküre) protects the fierce virtue of Brunnhild with a girdle of fire. Unfortunately M. Chevillard presents this fairy tale without any setting, and one sees a nice decorous gentleman in a black suit brandishing Wotan's menacing spear in the face of a modest score. . . . It is disconcerting and not decorative. You will argue that there is the magic of the orchestra. . . . Is that enough, however Wagnerian one may be?'

At this point Debussy, convinced that such an opera needs to be seen as well as heard, timidly suggests that the cinematograph should collaborate with Wagner and infuse some life into this childish tale for the benefit of the audience: 'One must move with the times, and we have no right to deprive Wagner of this discovery from which the music-halls get wonderful results in decidedly less worthy causes.'

The libretto of 'Parsifal' was also made a subject for jokes: 'Observe Amfortas, the mournful knight of the Grail, complaining like a modiste and whining like a baby. . . . A knight of the Grail, the son of a king, should run himself through rather than carry an unworthy wound around through melancholy cantilenas, and that during three acts. As for Kundry, that aged rose of hell, she has furnished Wagnerian literature with much copy. I confess I have but little love for this cold-blooded, sentimental hag. The finest character in "Parsifal" is Klingsor (former

Knight of the Grail, who was turned out of the Holy Place because he held opinions of his own on the subject of chastity). He is wonderful in his vengeful hatred. He knows what men are worth, and weighs the solidity of their vows of chastity in scales of contempt. From this one may safely argue that this cunning magician, this hardened old lag, is not merely the only human character, but the only normal character in this drama which contains the falsest of moral and religious theories—theories of which the youthful Parsifal is the heroic and foolish champion. In fact, in this Christian drama, no one wants to sacrifice himself (sacrifice is, nevertheless, one of the finest of Christian virtues); and if Parsifal finds his miraculous lance again, it is thanks to old Kundry, the real victim of this story, doubly a victim, sacrificed to the diabolical manœuvres of a Klingsor and the pious peevishness of the Knights of the Grail. . . .'

Debussy admits that 'the foregoing only refers to the poet, commonly admired in Wagner'. On one occasion at least he took exception to the artist in a general way, contrasting him with other German masters. It was in *Gil Blas* of January 19th, 1903, in connexion with a declaration unwisely formulated by Ludwig Ferdinand of Bavaria. The megalomaniac prince, who played in the orchestra at the big Wagnerian representations in Munich, had acclaimed Wagner as the greatest musician of his country. Debussy was furious with this kinsman of Ludwig II, whom he considers 'more a prince than an authority on music'. He protests vehemently, recalling Bach, Mozart, Beethoven, and scoffs at the opinion of his

Royal Highness with a bluntness that is anything but courtierlike: 'What about Bach? Was he just a man who had lots of children? Beethoven? Another nobody who was so bad-tempered that he decided to become deaf the better to annoy his contemporaries with his last quartets. And Mozart? He was merely a little libertine who wrote "Don Juan" to aggravate the Germans. But, lo and behold Germany's true glory, beside which but few names can stand!'

The discussion is carried to the arena of nationality. What influence was exercised on the art of his country by this man who is exalted by some above all others? Wagner led, or rather precipitated, German music into a blind alley: 'Wagner was never of service to music. He never even served Germany, for at the present time she is struggling in a tetralogical atmosphere where some are blinded by the last rays of this setting sun whilst others cling wildly to the neo-Beethovenian formula bequeathed by Brahms. And when Wagner, in a gesture of mad pride, cried: "And now, you have an art!" he might just as well have said: "And now I leave you the void. Find your way out of it as well as you can." There is no question of discussing Wagner's genius here. It is a dynamic force whose effects have been all the more certain because they were prepared by the hand of a magician whom nothing daunted.' This same idea was expressed in a reply to an inquiry on the Germanic influence, initiated by the *Mercure de France* in 1903: 'Wagner was—if one may express oneself with some of the grandiloquence that becomes him—a beautiful sunset that was mistaken for a dawn.'

The question is elaborated. The French musician, feeling himself incapable of eradicating entirely the violent Wagnerian fever from which he himself had suffered, gives his opinion on Wagner's influence in general. It is an angry opinion, which seems to be prompted by a remnant of enthusiasm; its exaggeration culminates in an ironical smile: 'As a result of this influence music was for a long time subject to a species of fever which was incurable in the case of all those who had breathed its dank vapours. As one would overstrain a broken-down mare, so Wagner, by sheer tyranny and force of will, dragged music in the trail of his selfish desire for glory. It is perhaps to the agonized cries of music that is due the hold which Wagner exercised on contemporary minds—so easy is it to awaken in the most conspicuous consciences the secret desire to satisfy the lust for crime.'

Wagnerians naturally get a liberal share of the inevitable lashes. Of all musical snobs they are the most fiercely scourged. In May, 1901, the Cirque d'Hiver celebrated a Wagner anniversary under the direction of Arthur Nikisch. Debussy was irritated by the excessive enthusiasm shown by the public: 'The most persistent delirium held the audience. God forgive me, but it was enough to make one believe that all those people were more or less natural offspring of Ludwig II of Bavaria.' He ridicules the snobbery which imposes the most tiresome performances on a very varied public:

' "Rhinegold" once more on the concert platform. Two and a half hours of music during which you are torn between a natural inclination to go away and a desire to go to sleep after having politely begged your neighbour to wake you at the last bar but one, so that you may duly applaud the masterly energy of M. Chevillard. Irony apart, this is the attitude of many well-bred people. They submit with more or less elegance to being bored, and if they do not go away it is because they must appear at the close, eloquent and well-informed. Otherwise, what object would they have in coming?'

If perchance Debussy asks that the 'Ring' be performed at the Opera, it is partly because 'we should thus be rid of it', but mostly because 'the pilgrims of Bayreuth would no longer worry us with their German gasconades'. This Wagnerian mania, which went through a series of evolutions until it embraced the whole fashionable world, got on the critic's nerves. Debussy gave his frank opinion when dealing with a performance of 'Parsifal' given in the spring of 1903 under the direction of Alfred Cortot and initiated by the very fashionable Société des Grandes Auditions. Owing no doubt to his 'Wagnerian iconoclasm' he did not receive an invitation. He was glad to forgo these elegant assemblies where 'the bright glory of the name inscribed on the programme enables those present to dispense with understanding, and makes it possible to listen attentively to the latest gossip or to admire that charming movement of the neck that women have, without paying any attention to the music'. His opinion was that such soirées risk making of Wagner's music a mere excuse for social gatherings:

'All things considered, that side of the Wagnerian art is annoying which first demanded that its followers should undertake expensive pilgrimages accompanied by mysterious rites. I know that Art-Religion was one of Wagner's favourite ideas; and that he was right, this being the best formula with which to detach and hold the imagination of a public—one, however, that turned out badly when it became a sort of Religion de Luxe which of necessity excluded many who are richer in goodwill than in coin. . . . The Société des Grandes Auditions, continuing its traditions of exclusiveness, seems to me to culminate in Art-Mondain (a detestable formula). When Wagner was in a good humour, he was wont to declare that he would never be so well understood as in France. Did he refer to purely aristocratic performances? I do not believe it. . . . (As it was, King Ludwig II of Bavaria worried him enough with questions of arbitrary etiquette.) His proud sensibility was too experienced not to know that true glory must be bestowed by the crowd and not by a more or less select and gilded audience. It is to be feared, therefore, that these performances, whose ostensible aim is the propagation of Wagnerian art, serve only to estrange it from the sympathy of the crowds—a roundabout way of making it unpopular. . . .'

In connexion with this example of society snobbishness, Debussy pronounced a general verdict on his adversary, Richard Wagner. This brief judgement summarizes calmly and with a certain suppressed emotion the contradictions of his articles: 'He can never quite die. He will eventually feel the cruel hand with which time destroys the most beautiful things. Some splendid ruins will, however, remain, in whose shade our grandchildren will dream of the past greatness of this man who, had he but been a little more human, would have been great for all time.'

This verdict, made up of love and hatred, was given once more by Debussy in more graphic, less definite terms which unite, whilst contrasting them, the names of Bach and Wagner: 'In conclusion, Wagner's work suggests a striking picture: Bach as the Holy Grail, Wagner as Klingsor wishing to crush the Grail and usurp its place.... Bach shines supreme over music, and in his goodness he has reserved for our hearing words as yet unknown, of the great lesson he has bequeathed us of disinterested love of music. Wagner disappears into the background.... He is fading away ... a black, disturbing shadow.'

In his final analysis Debussy's chief grievance against the great artist who degraded symphony to the service of his tragedies was a lack of this passion —disinterested love of music. For Debussy was above all a musician, whilst Wagner was above all a dramatist.

VIII

Foreign Music

THE foregoing chapters have shown that Claude Debussy, the so-called revolutionary of twenty years ago, was in reality a traditionalist. He delighted in old music, both foreign and French, and he would have wished the concert hall and the theatre to pay frequent homage to the masters of old. One day, in *Gil Blas*, without the least 'intention of contributing to the history of music', he suggested 'that it is perhaps a mistake to play the same things all the time, as it leads simple people to believe that music was born yesterday, whereas she has a Past whose ashes should be stirred. They hold within them that inextinguishable flame to which our Present will always owe a part of its splendour.' He wished that certain beautiful works of olden days might be saved from oblivion: 'Some dead men are really too discreet and wait too long for the pathetic reward of posthumous glory. Needless to say, none but reverent hands should lift the veil of death; but these exhumations are generally carried out by clumsy, jealous hands which, impelled by an unworthy and secret egoism, fling back to oblivion these poor flowers of the dead.' This love of old scores, which is so fervently shown in references to Rameau and French composers of the old régime, is no less keen in regard to Scarlatti, Bach, and Handel.

Here we have Alessandro Scarlatti with his hundred operas 'without counting all the other kinds of music. Heavens, how gifted must this man have been! How did he find time to live? . . . I don't know how this man found time to have a son and to make of him a distinguished clavecinist who is still appreciated to-day under the name of Domenico Scarlatti.'

Debussy writes in the most delicately elegant terms of a musical work by the father: 'We know a "Passion according to St. John" by him that is a little masterpiece of primitive grace: The choruses are written in a way suggesting the pale gold that encircled so charmingly the profile of virgins seen in frescoes of that time.' Handel is spoken of with less admiration: 'In truth, that monument of glory, J. S. Bach, hides from us Handel, whose oratorios, more numerous than the sands of the sea, are unknown. Like these too, they contain more pebbles than pearls. Nevertheless, with patience and goodwill, one would surely find interest in them.' Johann Sebastian Bach, the sovereign master 'in whom is all music', provokes enthusiasm—indeed paeans of praise.

In the third article published in the *Revue Blanche* Debussy wrote an account of a Good Friday concert in the course of which the violinist, Ysaÿe, had played Bach's Concerto in G. The orchestral performance went 'with a loud and painful tread. One would think from the heavy manner of its interpretation that Bach was being called upon to carry the weight of the centuries that have accumulated on his work.' Fortunately, Ysaÿe played the solo part 'as he alone perhaps is capable of doing it, without appearing to intrude. He has that freedom of expression, that unaffected beauty of tone which are essential to the interpretation of this music.' The Concerto is 'an admirable work among so many others already inscribed in the manuscripts of the great Bach'. Twelve years later Debussy again praised the grandeur of the slow movement: 'The andante of J. S. Bach's violin Concerto is so beautiful that in truth one no longer knows where to place oneself nor how to make oneself worthy to hear it. It haunts us long afterwards; and on coming out into the streets we are surprised that the sky is not bluer and that the Parthenon does not rise up before us. The fierce hooters of the motor buses soon bring us back to earth.' The same unreserved admiration is shown for the Mass in B minor. According to Debussy this music, like Goethe's second 'Faust', is of supreme grandeur: 'These works will remain monuments of beauty as unique as they are inimitable. Their influence is akin to that of the sea or the sky. They are not essentially German but are universal.'

What is that peculiar joy, that heavenly joy that is felt on hearing such music? It is pure joy, unalloyed by literature or sentiment, due to some extent to the contemplation of a work of art that is an outstanding example in line, ornament, and decoration. Debussy is carried away by the free play of sounds with their parallel or contrary curves. He is in ecstasy before the efflorescence of the adorable arabesque: 'There you find, almost intact, . . . the musical arabesque, or rather, that principle of ornamentation which is the basis of every mode of art. (The word "ornament" here has no connexion with the meaning given it in musical grammars.) The primitives—Palestrina, Vittoria, Orlando di Lasso, &c. . . . made use of this divine arabesque. They found the principle on which it is based in Gregorian chant, and supported its delicate interlacings with firm counterpoint. Bach in taking over the arabesque made it more supple, more fluid, and in spite of the severe discipline which this great Master imposed on Beauty, she was able to move freely with that ever-changing, ever-new fantasy which still surprises us to this day.'

Debussy defines the nature of his emotion: 'In Bach's music it is not the character of the melody that moves us, but its curve. Oftener still it is the parallel movement of several lines whose meeting, be it fortuitous or unanimous, calls forth emotion. In this ornamental conception, music reacts on the public and suggests images with machine-like precision. . . .' This really pure musician remains natural and noble: 'Do not imagine something outside Nature or artificial. It is, on the contrary, infinitely *truer* than the poor little human cries to which lyrical drama tries to give utterance. Above all, such music retains all its nobility. It never condescends to pander to that desire for sentimentality affected by people who are by way of being *so fond of music*. From superior heights it forces their respect if not their adoration.'[1]

'This ornamental conception having completely disappeared; music having been successfully domes-

[1] See Chapter II, page 12, of this volume.

ticated'—it will not therefore appeal to the public so easily as forms of music in which the expression is more direct; and Debussy takes advantage of the occasion to contrast the godlike Bach with his compatriot Wagner: 'We need not hesitate to say that we have never heard people whistling Bach. . . . Wagner will not have lacked this particular form of glory. On the boulevard, at the hour when the prisoners de luxe are released from musical houses of detention, one sometimes hears the "Spring Song" or the opening phrase of the "Meistersinger" gaily whistled. I am well aware that to many people this is all the glory that music need expect. One may nevertheless be allowed to hold a contrary opinion without appearing singular.'

Debussy did not often write of Mozart, but twice he praised this pure musician in brief terms of delight. Concerning one of his concertos 'which it is impossible to play badly, so well is it written for the piano', and of the Symphony in E flat which 'seemed a thing of luminous lightness, like a group of pretty children laughing joyously in the sunshine'.

On the other hand, Beethoven furnishes material for several articles. His works, particularly the symphonies, somewhat overburdened programmes, so Debussy considered. We have already quoted his dogmatic statements regarding the symphonic form adopted by the German master. His paradoxical criticism of the 'Pastoral Symphony' has often been quoted and keenly discussed. It was written after a performance at the Concerts Lamoureux. Weingartner had conducted the symphony 'with the care of a meticulous gardener. It was so neatly cleared of caterpillars that it gave the impression of a landscape varnished with a brush, the gentle undulations of the hills being represented by plush at ten francs a metre, and the trees crimped with curling tongs.' The excessive detail of this interpretation helped, perhaps, to provoke the critic's ill humour.

His mockery and censure have their origin in an intense love of nature: 'In short, the popularity of the "Pastoral Symphony" is due to the misunderstanding which not commonly exists between nature and man. Notice the scene by the stream! . . . a stream where the oxen apparently come to drink (or so the bassoons lead me to suppose), not to mention the wooden nightingale and the Swiss cuckoo which belong rather to the art of M. de Vaucanson[1] than to nature. . . . All this is useless imitation or a purely arbitrary interpretation. How much more deeply is the beauty of a landscape expressed in some pages of this old master, and this simply because there is no direct imitation, but merely a transposition of his feeling for all that is *invisible* in nature. Can one render the mystery of a forest by measuring the height of the trees? Is it not rather its unfathomable depths that appeal to the imagination? Besides, in this symphony Beethoven is dependent upon a period when nature was observed only through books. . . . This is apparent in the storm which forms part of this same symphony, where the terror

[1] A famous maker of mechanical toys (1709–82) [translator's note].

of beings and things is cloaked in romance though the thunder that growls is not very alarming.'

Ten years later there appeared another ironic criticism of this imitation of nature. The 'Pastoral Symphony' 'certainly remains one of the best examples of mechanical expression. . . . To hear an orchestra imitate the cries of animals is a real joy to young and old. To assist at a storm from an arm-chair is sheer sybaritism.' Thanks to Gabriel Pierné's charming interpretation, 'we were really in the country. The trees did not wear white ties; the stream, beside which the most German of idylls takes place, was delightfully fresh. A little more and we should have smelt the cowshed!'

Debussy, fearing that his mockery might be misinterpreted, is careful, before concluding his article of 1903, to introduce a note of admiration: 'It would be absurd to think that I am wanting in respect to Beethoven, but a musician of his genius could err more blindly than another.... No man is expected to write only masterpieces; and if the "Pastoral Symphony" is classed as such, the term loses force when applied to his other works. That is all I mean to say.'

The title of masterpiece is, in Debussy's opinion, wholly deserved by the 'Ninth Symphony'. He writes of it with reasoned enthusiasm. He even rejects the charge of lengthiness which authorities on music have brought against certain parts of the symphony. In the first place he deplores the mass of literature which the great work has called forth: 'The Choral Symphony has been enveloped in a fog of words and high-sounding epithets. This work and the famous Mona Lisa smile (which has been for ever labelled "mysterious") are the two masterpieces about which the greatest amount of nonsense has been written. The wonder is that it has not been buried under the heap of prose it called forth. Wagner proposed to complete its orchestration; others planned to explain its story by means of descriptive tableaux. In short, this clear, powerful work was turned into a bogy for the public. Presuming that there is a mystery in this symphony, it might perhaps be elucidated,—but to what purpose?'

Here is the actual critique, full of musicianship and feeling: 'Beethoven was not in the least literary. (At least, not in the sense now attached to this word.) He loved music with pride. Music was to him the passion, the joy, so painfully lacking in his private life. The Choral Symphony should perhaps be regarded as merely a more unbounded gesture of musical pride—nothing more. A little note-book, in which are noted down more than two hundred different aspects of the main theme of the finale of this symphony, bears witness to the persistent research, the purely musical speculation which directed it. (Schiller's verses have really only a sonorous value.) He wished this idea to contain its own inevitable development; and apart from its marvellous intrinsic beauty, it is magnificent in its fulfilment of his expectations. There exists no more triumphant example of the adaptability of an idea to the mould that is designed for it. At every advance there is new joy, achieved without weariness, without apparent repetition, suggesting the budding of a fabulous tree whose leaves all burst forth at once. In spite of its huge proportions, there is nothing superfluous in this work—not even the Andante which, according to recent critics, is long drawn out. Does it not constitute a rest, arranged with delicate forethought between the rhythmic persistence of the scherzo and the rushing instrumental torrent leading the voices triumphantly to the glory of the finale? Besides, Beethoven had written eight symphonies; the figure 9 must therefore have impressed itself upon his mind with an almost fatalistic significance, and Beethoven laboured to surpass himself. I do not see how any one could doubt that he succeeded. The human feeling which bursts through the customary bounds of the symphony springs from a soul panting for freedom, a soul which, by the irony of fate, dashes itself against the gilded bars fashioned by the unkind friendship of the great. Beethoven must have suffered intensely and burned with the desire for communion with humanity. Hence the cry addressed by the thousand voices of his genius to the humblest and poorest of his brethren. Was he heard by them? . . . A disturbing question, this.'

Beethoven's orchestration is excellent in the opinion of Debussy, or rather, of Monsieur Croche, who contrasts it with that of Wagner: 'Beethoven's orchestra, which appears to him a formula in black and white, resulting in the whole exquisite gamut of greys; that of Wagner which is a species of polychromatic putty, spread almost uniformly, in which he assured me he could no longer distinguish the sound of a violin from that of a trombone.'

On the other hand, Monsieur Croche does not approve of the way the sonatas are written for the piano, for they exceed the scope of the instrument: 'Beethoven's piano sonatas are very badly written for the piano. The later ones in particular are rather transcriptions from orchestral scores. A third hand is often required, and this Beethoven must have realized—at least, I hope he did.'

Apart from the greater works, Debussy wrote only of the song 'Adelaïde', which an artist had sung 'with an elegant tremolo'. This page he considers unworthy of its author: 'I think the old master must have forgotten to burn this melody, and the over-cupidity of his heirs is probably to blame for the mistake of its exhumation.' This lack of reverence need not astonish us. Debussy admired Beethoven as he admired Wagner, but as he stated one day: 'I refuse to admire them *en bloc* because I have been told that they are Masters! That, never! In my opinion, the attitude that people adopt towards Masters nowadays is unpleasantly servile. If a dull page annoys me, I insist on my right to say so, whoever its author may be. . . .'

Beethoven, Mozart, Bach, are three sovereign masters, differing one from the other by reason of development in taste: 'Genius can, of course, dispense with taste: of this Beethoven is an example. Mozart on the other hand, his equal in genius, has, in addition, the most delicate taste. Take the work of J. S. Bach, that benevolent god, to whom musicians should offer a prayer before setting to work so that they may be preserved from mediocrity. We shall seek in vain for one fault in taste in all that vast amount of work in which we constantly find things that might have been written yesterday, from the capricious arabesque to that outpouring of religious feeling for which we have so far found no better expression.'

Out of the whole German romantic movement of the nineteenth century Debussy seems to have appreciated the work of only one musician—Weber. There is no one whose memory he has evoked with more affectionate, more tender admiration, and whose powerful qualities he has extolled in more moving terms. Georges Hüe's opera, 'Titania', of which he was to give an account, reminded him of an exquisite drama—'A Midsummer-Night's Dream', and so, of 'Oberon'. Forthwith he leaves aside the work of the French composer, and speaks no other word of him. An image takes possession of the critic's mind to the exclusion of everything else, that of 'a man more or less forgotten, at least by the theatre. I used to see him in the streets of London, dragging along a body worn out by the keen intellect; his brow radiant with the light that is in those who have had beautiful visions. He went his way sustained by a feverish desire not to die until he had heard that last work in which is the painful fever of the last drops of his blood. What great effort produced once more this fiery abandon, these romantic rhythms which had so spontaneously proclaimed his youthful genius? No one will ever know. . . . This work contained that dreamy melancholy so peculiar to the period, and was never weighed down by that crude German moonlight in which most of his contemporaries indulged. He was, perhaps, the first man to occupy himself with the relation that should exist between the multiple soul of nature and the soul of man. He certainly conceived the idea of utilizing legend, realizing the supernatural qualities the music would find therein. In truth, music alone has the power to evoke at will unreal scenes, to call up that unquestioned but fantastic world which has its secret being in the mysterious poetry of the night, in those thousand nameless sounds of leaves caressed by the rays of the moon. Every means of describing the fantastic in terms of music we find in the brain of this man. Even the rich orchestral experimentation of our own times has not surpassed him to any great extent. Those who would reproach him with a weakness for ostentation and for florid arias must remember that he married a singer. He probably adored her—the excuse is none the less powerful for being sentimental. In spite of his matrimonial leanings which led him to tie semiquavers into elegant bows of ribbon, he frequently expressed beautiful and simple human feeling in accents free from useless flourishes. You will all have recognized in this man, Karl Maria von Weber.'

The masterpieces of this forgotten or neglected musician-dramatist—'Oberon', 'Freischütz', 'Euryanthe', earned for him the title of father of the Romantic School 'to which we owe our Berlioz, whose intense love for romantic colouring sometimes caused him to forget music; Wagner, the great maker of symbols; and, nearer to us, Richard Strauss, whose imagination is so curiously adapted to romanticism. Weber may be proud of such descendants, and the glory of these children of his genius should console him for the fact that only the overtures to the above-mentioned works are now played.' Debussy wrote the following enthusiastic lines on the overture to 'Freischütz' which was played with passionate feeling, 'as it should be', under the conductorship of Chevillard: 'The sonorous arrangement of this overture is amazing, and the return to the key of C major (the original key) produces one of those emotions which never lose in intensity or novelty. It is good stuff and wears well. Of that there is no doubt.'

Chopin too is well beloved. His charming soul is reflected in 'Tristan and Isolde', 'here and there in the music, directing its passion'. Chopin was 'a man whose generous ideas were never bartered for the one hundred per cent. profit which is the highest ambition of some of our Masters'. His nervous temperament lacked the patience essential to the composition of a sonata, and those he produced were rather highly developed sketches. He did, however, inaugurate an individual treatment of this form, not to mention the delicious musical quality with which he endowed it.

During the war Debussy undertook to revise Chopin's works for a French edition. In this connexion he wrote a brief preface in which he expresses his deep admiration and great love for the Polish master: 'Chopin's music is amongst the most beautiful ever written. To acknowledge this in 1915 is but an inadequate tribute. It does not dispense one from commenting on the significance of Chopin's music and the influence it has never ceased to exert on contemporary music. Because of the very nature of his genius it is impossible to classify him. Field's purely epochal influence was slight. His Italianism and his chromaticism, which have met with varied criticism, are but the outward expression of an acute sensibility and are peculiarly characteristic of him. Chopin was a delightful narrator of legends of love or war which often take flight towards the forest of "As You Like It", where the fairies alone hold sway over our minds. The freedom of his form deceived his commentators just as the many brilliant passages suggest the virtuoso; but one should nevertheless appreciate the sure and skilful use he makes of them. . . .'

Weber's immediate successors, Schubert and Mendelssohn, are not kindly treated. Debussy refers to a much-played symphony of Schubert which 'cannot make up its mind to remain unfinished once and for all'. He does not appreciate the songs and indeed he goes so far as to compare them to certain chansonnettes from the 'Chat Noir': 'These lieder are inoffensive . . . they smell of the chest of drawers of some nice, provincial old maids . . . dried flowers . . . photographs that are dead indeed . . . ! The effect is repeated through endless verses; and by the time the third is reached one begins to wonder if the time has not come to produce our own Paul Delmet.'

In his formal mention of Mendelssohn his contempt is barely veiled. His 'Reformation Symphony', played at the Concerts Lamoureux on the same day as a bad concerto by the pianist Émile Sauer, was one of the 'two altogether annoying moments during the concert'. How did Schumann allow his pure genius to be influenced by this 'facile and elegant notary'? The influence is particularly noticeable in 'Faust'. There 'one often stumbles on Mendelssohn. I prefer unadulterated Mendelssohn, because then one knows what to expect.' Not even as a writer of songs does Schumann escape Debussy's criticisms: 'Musicians', so the French master believed, 'understand nothing about poetry and should not set it to music. They only succeed in spoiling it. . . . Schumann never understood Heinrich Heine. At least, that is my impression. He may have been a great genius, but he could not grasp all the fine irony that is in Heine. Notice, for instance, how he misses the point in the "Dichterliebe".'

It is evidently Mendelssohn, the impeccable notary, that Debussy had in mind when, in connexion with Liszt's 'Mazeppa' he declares that he prefers the careless genius of the illustrious virtuoso to formal perfection: 'This symphonic poem (Mazeppa) is full of the worst faults; sometimes it is even vulgar, and yet the tumultuous passion which never ceases to agitate it ends by gripping you with such force that you find yourself liking it and make no further effort to explain to yourself why. . . . (One may assume a disgusted expression on leaving, because it is the right thing to do! Pure hypocrisy, believe me.) The undeniable beauty of Liszt's work is I believe due to the fact that he loved music to the exclusion of every other sentiment. If at times he addresses her with undue familiarity and takes her unceremoniously on his knees, this method is at least as good as the affectation of those who behave as though they had just met her for the first time. Their behaviour is certainly very proper, but it lacks fire. The fire and abandon to which Liszt's genius frequently attains are preferable to the white-gloved perfection.'

A successor of Liszt who has become the most remarkable representative of musical Germany, Richard Strauss, inspired Debussy with a lively admiration and a degree of sympathy which contrast strongly with his violent disparagement of Wagner, examples of which are to be found in a special chapter. His admiration and sympathy are perhaps due, at least in part, to the absence of Wagnerism in the works of Strauss. He considers him as 'an exceptional example of German musical thought. As regards orchestration, is not his formula an amplification of that of Liszt? Does he not remind us of Berlioz in his fondness for emphasizing with philosophical narrative the plot of his symphonic poems? At any rate, there is no Wagnerian influence.' On another occasion Debussy makes the same observation in different terms: 'He is about the only original musician of young Germany. He resembles Liszt in the remarkable skill of his orchestral work, and our Berlioz in his anxiety to prop up his music with literature.'

In 1903 Debussy gave an account of three great works of Richard Strauss: 'Till Eulenspiegel',

'Heldenleben', and 'Italien'. The first had previously been played in 1901 under the direction of Nikisch. 'This piece', the critic of the *Revue Blanche* remarks, 'resembles "An hour of music in an asylum". Clarinets describe crazy parabolas; trumpets are so absolutely muted and stopped up that the horns, foreseeing a latent sneeze, hasten to reply with the customary "God bless you!", a big drum contributes its boum-boum, appearing to emphasize the kicks of the clowns. You do not know whether to roar with laughter or with pain, and you wonder at finding things in their customary places. For if the double-basses blew through their bows, if the trombones rubbed their instruments with an imaginary bow, and if M. Nikisch were discovered seated on the knees of an attendant, it would not seem at all extraordinary. But in spite of all this there is genius in certain aspects of the work, notably in the amazing sureness of the orchestration and in that frenzied movement which sweeps us on from beginning to end, making us live through all the hero's adventures. . . .'

Two years later he republished this amusing critique almost word for word. It was on the occasion of a concert given by Strauss himself. In this poem, he added, 'there is no doubt as to the anecdotes the music endeavours to tell and the likeness of the orchestra to the crazy illustrations of a text'. He sums up his observations thus: 'The art of Strauss is certainly not always so definitely fantastic; but he undoubtedly thinks in coloured pictures and he seems to outline his thoughts by means of the orchestra. The method is unusual and not hackneyed.

In addition Strauss employs it to carry out the development in a manner peculiarly his own. It is not the severe architectural manner of Bach or Beethoven, but a development in rhythmic colours. With amazing sangfroid he superimposes on one another tonalities that are utterly unrelated. He does not care in the least whether or not they are nerve-racking, he only aims at making them alive.'

All these peculiarities are carried to their highest intensity in 'Heldenleben'. 'Certain ideas may not appeal to us in their initial stages because they verge on the commonplace or are exaggeratedly Italian in style, but after a moment we are gripped, first by the prodigious variety of the orchestral effects, then by a frenzied movement which carries us completely away. We lose control of our emotions. We do not even notice that this symphonic poem oversteps the limits which patience usually concedes to this form of music. Once more it is a book of pictures, it even suggests the cinematograph. . . . But we must admit that the man who constructed such a work with such continuity of effort is not far from being a genius.'

Debussy discovered the promise of the future independence of Richard Strauss in an early work of his. This was 'Italien', a fantasy whose developments appeared to him rather long and obvious, but the third part of which, 'En Rade de Sorrente', fascinated him by the beauty of its colouring. He regrets having heard only an excerpt—and that unaccompanied by any explanatory note—of the opera 'Feuersnot': 'This scene lost much by being taken from its setting, and as the programme gave no explanation, its plan was quite incomprehensible. One particular episode, which roused a veritable orchestral torrent, seemed very formidable for a love-scene! In the drama this torrent is probably justified. This might perhaps give the opera-houses an opportunity for staging something new.'

The conclusion is full of admiration: Strauss must have got from Nietzsche 'his fine contempt for silly sentimentalities and his wish that music, instead of being content to illuminate our nights more or less successfully, might rather aim at replacing the sun. I can assure you that there is sunshine in the music of Richard Strauss.'

The performance of 'Tod und Verklärung' at the Concerts Colonne towards the end of 1912 called forth less praise if not veiled censure. He first remarks on a 'curious analogy between the art of Boecklin and the art of Richard Strauss. . . . The same indifference to a preconceived plan, the same bent for seeking form directly in colour and drawing from this same colour picturesque dramatic effects.' He then indulges in satire on the subject of the so-called symphonic poem: 'In the "Cuisinière Bourgeoise", the paragraph entitled "Civet de lièvre" says, "First take a hare! . . ." Richard Strauss proceeds differently. To make a symphonic poem he takes any idea that occurs to him, thus proving himself to be an extraordinary illusionist who could give points to the most adept of Fakirs. Although "Tod und Verklärung" has not the sparkling sureness of "Till Eulenspiegel" or the passionate grandiloquence of "Don Juan", yet it contains formulas that always remained dear to Richard Strauss, although he subsequently improved upon them. The beginning suggests the atmosphere of the sepulchre in which alarming larvae appear to move; the soul engages in terrible struggles, endeavouring to free itself from the vile body which still holds it to earth. But here an oboe sings a cantilena with Italian inflexions. The reason for this is not at first obvious, because we have failed to keep in mind those countless migrations of souls so fraught with mystery. Besides, if people insist on wanting to understand what happens in a symphonic poem, we may as well give up writing them. The frequent misunderstandings that occur between composer and listener will certainly not be dissipated by reading those little guide-books in which the letters of the alphabet represent parts of picture puzzles, which you try to solve during the performance. And yet, the "Transfiguration" takes place before the eyes of the public, without any apparent trickery beyond the great chords in C major. It is this key which most perfectly conveys the impression of eternity. That does not necessarily mean that music moves with greater ease on the superhuman than on the merely human plane. That idea is artificial and generally of literary origin. Besides, in this case there is no need for a programme which offers ever-recurring temptation for verbose explanations. Music simple and unadorned suffices. That is why in "Tod und Verklärung" certain parts appear somewhat empty, as though they no longer justified the title. No one is to blame for that, not even Richard Strauss, who is one of the most dominant geniuses of our time.'

In spite of its reservations, Debussy's praise of Richard Strauss is all the more valuable because he is not lenient towards other contemporary German musicians. Brahms he only mentioned casually, in connexion with his neo-Beethovenism and his violin concerto, which Debussy considered 'very tiresome'. For Siegfried Wagner he has no pity: 'M. Siegfried Wagner carries with ease the heavy heritage of glory left by his illustrious father. . . . He does not even appear to be aware of it, for his dry, meticulous manner is full of calm assurance. He greatly resembles his father, but the thumb-mark of genius which stamps the original is absent in the reproduction. . . . In his youth he was, apparently, destined for architecture. We shall never know if architecture lost much by his having branched off into music. Neither can we be sure that the latter has gained thereby. Certainly, his determination to continue what his father had commenced proves him a respectful son, but one cannot do these things as easily as one might take over a hosiery shop. It is not that Siegfried Wagner fails to realize how infinitely his father's work is beyond him, but that his having disregarded this fact can only be ascribed to a sentiment made up of the most childish vanity and the desire to honour a beloved memory by a dedicatory work. Besides, it would have been difficult for him to escape the spell of Bayreuth, and not to try to drink the dregs of the old magician's cup. Unfortunately, only the lees of the magic draught remained, and these taste of vinegar. These reflections came to me as I listened to fragments of "Graf Wildfang", a musical comedy in three acts by S. Wagner. It is honest music, nothing more; like the task of a student who had studied under Richard Wagner but about whom the latter had bothered but little.'

At the Concerts Lamoureux, Siegfried Wagner had conducted, among other works, the delightful 'Treppenmusik' with which his father had celebrated the joyful event of his birth: 'In the performance of the "Siegfried Idyll", which indeed he conducts admirably, M. Wagner should perhaps have listened to the persuasive counsels of the parental love with which this work is imbued. This music bade him go through life free and joyous, not soliciting a glory that can only prove deceptive. It murmured his name, and surrounded it with a light that was to shine for ever. Why did he aspire to a greater brilliance which will remain problematic and which, in spite of everything, will leave him what is, in my opinion, his only enviable title—that of son of Richard Wagner? Still, the soul of another is a dim forest where one must walk with care. Siegfried Wagner must be moved by stronger reasons than those which I offer in explanation. . . .'

What was known twenty-five years ago as 'the young Russian school' is, needless to say, extolled by Debussy with the keenest enthusiasm. Like all Frenchmen, Debussy disapproves of Tchaikovsky, but Rimsky-Korsakof and Mussorgsky called forth his ardent praise. His opinion on Mussorgsky has frequently been quoted and deserves to be reproduced in full.

It is on the subject of the 'Nursery', a series of songs with piano accompaniment: 'This title is given to a suite of seven songs each of which is a scene of childhood, and is a masterpiece. Mussorgsky is little known in France, but that is excusable, for he is no better known in Russia. He was born at Karevo, in Central Russia, in 1839. He died in 1881, in the Nicholas Military Hospital at St. Petersburg. It is apparent from these dates that to become a genius he had little time to lose. He lost none, and he will leave an indelible impression on the minds of those who love him or will come to love him. No one has ever appealed to the best that is in us in deeper or more tender accents. He is unique and will remain so, for his art is free from artifice or arid formula. Never was refined sensibility interpreted by such simple means. It is like the art of an inquisitive savage who discovers music at every step made by his emotions. Neither is there ever question of any definite form; or rather, this form is so manifold that it cannot possibly be likened to the recognized or orthodox forms. It is achieved by little consecutive touches linked by a mysterious bond and by his gift of luminous intuition. Sometimes too, Mussorgsky produced the effect of shuddering, restless shadows which close around us and fill the heart with anguish.'

Following on this general criticism is an analysis of three pieces in the collection: 'In the "Nursery", we have the prayer of a little girl before she goes to sleep. In it he describes the gestures, the delicate scruples of a child's soul, and even the delightful way little girls have of posing as grown-ups, all expressed in accents of ardent sincerity which are found nowhere else. The "Doll's Lullaby" seems to have been interpreted word for word, thanks to marvellous powers of assimilation and to that faculty for imagining fairy landscapes which is peculiar to the mind of a child. The end of this lullaby is so soft, so sleep-inducing, that the little girl falls asleep over her own stories. There is also the terrible little boy, riding astride a stick, who transforms the room into a battle-field, breaking now the arm, now the leg of poor defenceless chairs. By and by injuries are of a more personal nature. Then there are screams, tears, and all the fun is over! . . . But the damage was not serious . . . two seconds on Mother's knee, the kiss that cures, and . . . the battle begins afresh, whilst once more the chairs don't know where to hide themselves.'

This literary transcription of the most animated music imaginable is itself full of life. The purely technical appreciation is contained in a few words: 'I should like to emphasize the fact that the little dramas are all written with the greatest simplicity. Mussorgsky is content with a chord which Monsieur . . . (I forget his name) would consider inadequate, or a modulation so spontaneous that to Monsieur . . . (the same) it would be an unknown quantity.' Debussy expected to have occasion to speak of Mussorgsky again. The opportunity, however, did not occur, but in a conversation published in 1911 he repeated his admiration for this 'god of music'.

His opinion of Rimsky-Korsakof is little known. In 1903 the Concerts Lamoureux had played the 'Antar Symphony', 'in fiery fashion. The beauty of this symphony was never more admirably rendered, besides, it is a pure masterpiece wherein Rimsky-Korsakof renovates the customary symphony form whilst incidentally casting it aside. It would be impossible to describe the charm of the themes, the dazzling orchestral and rhythmic effects. I defy any one to remain insensible to the spell of this music, it makes one forget life, one's neighbour in the stalls, and even the desirability of maintaining a correct attitude. You just want to shout for joy. With difficulty you limit yourself to making an absurd noise with your hands, but that is certainly poor thanks to a man who has given you moments of happiness.'

He confessed that he knew nothing of the works of the younger Russians. Not even during his journey to Russia, in December 1913, was the opportunity afforded him to get acquainted with any of their works. On the other hand, he was enabled to appraise the music of Stravinsky. He hailed this composer's début in Paris and praised the 'delightful originality' of 'The Fire-Bird'. He thought very highly of Stravinsky's innovatory tendencies, his keen instinct, his eager and acute curiosity.

Debussy gave his opinion of two Scandinavian composers. To one of them, Delius, he devotes but a few lines; to the other, Grieg, almost an entire feuilleton in *Gil Blas*. The 'Poèmes Danois' by

Delius, for voice and orchestra, 'are', he states, 'very soft, very colourless songs, suitable for singing wealthy convalescents to sleep. . . . There is always a note that clings to a chord, like a water-lily on a lake, tired of the moon's gaze, or . . . a little balloon blocked by the clouds.'

The article devoted to Grieg opens with a political reference—(in 1903 the Norwegian musician's concert had been somewhat disturbed owing to demonstrations connected with the Dreyfus Affair). Then follows a thumb-nail sketch of Grieg as a conductor: 'His front view suggests a photographer of genius. Seen from the back, the way in which he wears his hair makes him look like those plants called sunflowers, dear to parrots and to the gardens of small provincial stations. In spite of his age, he is vivacious and wiry, and he conducts with a nervous attention to detail which emphasizes every nuance and distributes the emotion with unwearying care.'

Following on this introduction comes a complete account of the concert, except the 'ouverture pour couloir', which hardly any one had been able to listen to owing to the tumult of conflicting demonstrations. The songs, concerto, and orchestral suite are discussed. The songs must have made the same impression on him as had the pleasant songs of Delius three years before, for in the middle of the criticism we find the selfsame words repeated: 'There is little to be said of the first two; they are Grieg à la Schumann. The third, "Le Cygne", is more sophisticated (it is also a drawing-room favourite). In this orchestral cuisine the savour of the harps mingles with the lemon flavour of the oboes, the whole being steeped in the juice of the stringed instruments. There are pauses too which thrill the audience, and so we have the unfailing formula of the encore. It is a very gentle kind of song, very colourless,—music suitable for sending wealthy convalescents to sleep. There is always a note that clings to a chord, like a water-lily on a lake, tired of the moon's gaze, or . . . a little balloon blocked by the clouds. This music is so ineffably charming that it is irresistible. It was enthusiastically encored, thanks to that fine old French sensibility which can always be counted on. Mme Gulbranson sang these three songs in a voice that was now light, now dreamy, and contained the cold, distinguished melancholy of the fiords which are Norway's greatest beauty.'

There is applause. 'It is Pugno of the Beautiful Hands. When you see Pugno, you may know that Grieg's concerto is not far off. . . . He plays it effectively, and no one gets from it better effects than he. With almost incredible skill he saves it from appearing commonplace and artificial. One no longer notices that this concerto, which begins with Schumann and ends with an apotheosis worthy of "Excelsior",[1] has very little individuality. His treatment of the piano is quite in tradition, and I have never understood why he breaks in here and there with blasts of warlike trumpets which usually announce the beginning of a little cantabile passage that sends the audience into transports. (Trumpets! . . . your candour is abused.)'

In dealing with the 'Mélodies élégiaques' Debussy

[1] An old-fashioned ballet (translator's note).

gives a literary translation of Grieg's usual methods. This has often been quoted: 'How melodious are the two "Mélodies élégiaques" for stringed instruments! In the second particularly, one feels the influence of Massenet . . . (though it has not that voluptuous abandon which characterizes his music and makes one love it with a love that is almost forbidden). In the case of Grieg it is inclined to stretch, like the marshmallow sweetmeats sold at fairs and which the seller's hands have previously kneaded—this process being, it appears, absolutely essential to their success. In these two songs Grieg repeats once more the formulas which previously made his fortune. He begins with a little unpretentious phrase which travels its own little road. On the way it comes across harmonic flowers with which it adorns its artless beauty. Then the whole is transported a story higher with obligatory mute effects. Then it comes down again, and by a series of cadences, carefully side-tracked, it dies away in a ritardando. The transports are renewed . . . and in one's mouth there remains the delightful taste of a pink sweet filled with snow.'

Debussy prefers to these over-sophisticated songs 'Peer Gynt', the orchestral suite to Ibsen's drama: 'The ideas are charming and the rhythms ingenious; the emotion is more authentically Norwegian. The orchestration, too, is better balanced, and facile effects are replaced by original devices. This concert, which was devoted to Grieg, concluded, for some inexplicable reason, with the finale of the "Twilight of the Gods", sung by Mme Gulbranson. Search as I may, I can find no reason why this monolith of German art was placed beside the Norwegian melancholy of Grieg, and I left before. . . . One does not eat roast beef after sweets.'

The summing-up is severe: 'To come back to Grieg and conclude with him, as is proper, one regrets that his stay in Paris taught us nothing new about his art. In his treatment of the folk-music of his country he shows himself a sensitive musician, though he is far from turning it to such good account as do Balakiref and Rimsky-Korsakof the Russian folk-music. Apart from this he is but a clever musician, caring more for effect than for true art. His guiding spirit was, it seems, Richard Nordraak, a young man of his own age, a born genius who showed promise of becoming a great musician when he died at the age of twenty-four. His death is doubly to be regretted since it deprived Norway of glory and Grieg of a friendly influence which would certainly have prevented him from straying into treacherous paths. Grieg, like Solness, the Masterbuilder (one of Ibsen's last dramas), aims at building for the children of men a house where they will be at home and happy. . . . I found no trace of this fine ideal in what M. Grieg offered us yesterday. But we know nothing of his later works. They are, perhaps, the "happy homes" of which Ibsen speaks! In any case, M. Grieg did not afford us the pleasure of entering them. The enthusiastic reception tendered him yesterday should compensate him for having taken the trouble to come to France. Let us ardently hope that he may at some future time judge us worthy of finding ourselves, if not at home, at least happy in his music.'

Six weeks previous to this concert, Debussy had already given an unfavourable criticism of Grieg's concerto: 'Mme Teresa Carreño played a concerto by Grieg. In this connexion, have you ever noticed how insufferable people of the North become when they try to be Southern? The end of this concerto, which is reminiscent of Leoncavallo, is a surprising example of this fact. The piano emulates the "pifferari", and the orchestra seconds it with such truculence and such a blaze of colour that you are convinced that nothing can save you from sunstroke. But Mme Teresa Carreño is very talented—much more so than Grieg, who rather takes advantage of the fact that he is Norwegian.'

In this criticism as in his feuilleton in *Gil Blas*, Debussy's extreme severity was due to a very legitimate national feeling. Grieg had been 'anything but friendly towards France at the time of the "Affaire"', writing, as he did, 'irritably that he never again wished to set foot in a country where liberty was so misunderstood'. He conveniently 'wiped out the incident when he crossed the frontier to conduct this French orchestra which had formerly been the object of his Scandinavian contempt'. This exposed him to the severe judgement of those Frenchmen whose patriotism is sensitive to unseemly attacks. Eleven years later Debussy was again called upon to give an account of the works of Grieg. The few lines in which he did so were characterized by greater indulgence and even expressed sympathy and goodwill. He praised the 'engaging melancholy' of his colleague's work and the charm of certain pages. In poetic terms he admitted that 'this music has the icy freshness of his country's lakes, the breathless ardour of its sudden, early Spring'.

At the time when Debussy acted as musical critic, it was less usual than now to devote an entire concert to a foreign nation. In writing of modern Italian music, the operatic only was touched on. This, as we have already seen, he despised for its realism. In 1903 he heard an entire programme of Polish music, and in 1913 he assisted at an evening of Spanish music.

The impression left on him by the Polish music was not very definite: 'Up to the present, I have not a very clear feeling about it! In a competition open to all Polish composers, S. Stojowski's Symphony in D minor was awarded a prize offered by Paderewski. (It does not make one wish to hear the others.) We are told that it was applauded and acclaimed as a very important work. With your permission I shall adhere to this appreciation furnished by the programme. As for the rest, I quite admit that Noskowski's "Steppe" possesses animation and that one can see his Cossacks prance as they shout Apache cries. Mme Bolska sings very well, and the collar of M. Mlynarski, the conductor, grows limp in a worthy cause.'

In 1913 he devoted a highly appreciative article in 'S.I.M.' to 'Spanish music played by real Spaniards', that is, by the Symphonic Orchestra of Madrid under the conductorship of F. Arbos. This performance inevitably reminded him of an International

Exhibition where, in former days, he had enjoyed visiting certain booths in the Champ de Mars. In these ephemeral surroundings he had first become acquainted with Spanish folk-music. The concert conducted by Arbos was but a fresh proof of the influence which, within recent times and thanks to Debussy's own example, folk-lore wielded on Symphonists of the young ultramontane school.

The account starts with general remarks: 'To many it was something of a revelation, for it was practically unknown except from vague Exhibition memories. Curiosity drew us to "La Feria", and such names as "La Macarona", "La Soledad", were in themselves sufficient to awaken interest and to arouse enthusiasm which was not always entirely due to the music. However, one heard that admirable folk-music, so full of fancy and rhythm as to make it one of the richest in the world. This very richness appears to have been the cause of the tardy development of the other type of music. Professionals were shyly reluctant to enclose so many lovely improvisations in the bonds of formulas. For a long time they were content to write in the popular form those Zarzuelas in which the notes of the guitar rise from the street to the stage almost without a change. But the rugged beauty of the old Moorish cantilenas remained unforgettable, whilst the old traditions of Escobedo and Morales, masters of the great Vittoria who with him made the Spanish Renaissance famous, were forgotten. There was no reason why a change should be made . . . what more can be desired of a country where the very stones on the roads seem to blaze with a voluptuousness which burns the eyes, where the muleteers summon from their throats notes of sincerest passion. Why be astonished at the decadence of the last century? Indeed, why call it decadence, since the folk-music retained its beauty? Wise and blessed would those countries be that kept this wild flower jealously sheltered from administrative classical regulations. It was about this period that was formed that group of composers who were determined to turn to account the inestimable treasure that lay hidden in the songs of old Spain.'

Of the five composers whose works Debussy heard—Albeniz, Turina, Casas, del Campo, Arbos, he places Albeniz far above the others: 'Isaac Albeniz,' he writes, 'who was first known as an incomparable virtuoso, subsequently acquired a marvellous knowledge of the craft of composition. Although he does not in any way resemble Liszt, he reminds one of him in the generous lavishness of his ideas. He was the first to turn to account the harmonious melancholy, the peculiar humour of his native country (he was a Catalan). There are few works in music to compare with "El Albaicin" in the third book of "Iberia". It is redolent of the atmosphere of those Spanish evenings perfumed with carnations and "aguardiente". . . . It is like the muffled notes of a guitar lamenting in the night with sudden awakenings and nervous starts. Although in "El Albaicin" the popular themes are not exactly reproduced, it is the work of one who has absorbed them, listening till they have passed into his music, leaving no trace of a boundary line. "Eritana" in the fourth book of "Iberia" portrays the joy of morning, the happy discovery of an inn where the wine is cool. An ever-changing crowd passes, the rhythm of their laughter marked by the beat of the Basque tambourines. Never has music attained to such diverse, such colourful impressions. One's eyes close, dazzled by such wealth of imagery. There are many other things in this "Iberia" collection, wherein Albeniz has put what is best in him. They are written with a carefulness of composition that is almost exaggerated, thanks to a generous nature which went so far as to *throw music out the windows*.'

Debussy remarks that 'the other composers, though they do not surpass Albeniz, follow in the same path. But whilst the influences working on Albeniz were very definitely French, in the case of the others they appear to be German, at least in form.' This remark applies in particular to the 'Divina Commedia' by Conrado del Campo, which is akin to the poems of Richard Strauss in its powerful construction. He gives very sympathetic praise to the 'Procesión del Rocio' by Joaquin Turina and 'A mi Tierra' by Peres Casas. The former work is arranged like a beautiful fresco. Clear contrasts of light and shade make it easy to listen to in spite of its dimensions. J. Turina, like Albeniz, is strong on folk-music. There is still some uncertainty in his mode of development and he believes it useful to refer to illustrious musical contractors. J. Turina might well dispense with them and listen to more intimate voices. 'A mi Tierra' (To my Country), a

Murcian suite by Peres Casas, is full of a poetry that is redolent of Oriental languor. 'It contains some very novel orchestral combinations in which the persistent seeking after colour is nearly always justified by the sincerity of expression.'

In conclusion Debussy remarks with admiration that 'whilst all these works have their source in folk-music, they do not in any way resemble one another'; and he sees in this fact a striking proof of the infinite wealth of Spanish folk-lore. Indeed, some of his own works were to a certain extent inspired by this popular art; and, as we remarked above, he thus opened a new path in which the young Spaniards have resolutely followed him.

He liked the music of the young Hungarians, such as Bartók and Kodály, but considered that, in 1914, the moment had not come to assess the work of young men who were still seeking. Moreover, he could not admit that critics were justified in pouncing upon the music of youthful composers in order to dissect, classify, and judge it. Hasty judgement he considered as one of the plagues of modern times. At the end of 1913 he confessed that the time had come for him to concentrate, and that he had 'made it a rule to hear as little music as possible'.

He had heard no music by Schönberg. Having read what was being written about this composer, he decided to read a quartet of his, but was unable, he declared, to carry out his intention.

In May 1913 he had to speak of Futurist music. But this he did merely by way of registering a date. He had little faith in an art that 'aimed at uniting in an all-embracing symphony all the noises of modern capitals, from the strokes of the railway engines to the little trumpet by means of which the mender of china advertises his passage. The idea is quite practical so far as concerns the recruiting of the orchestra; but will this orchestra ever achieve the truly satisfying sonority of a metal factory in full work? Let us wait and see, and refrain from ridicule; we can imagine the effect that the final scene of the "Götterdämmerung" would produce upon a minstrel of yore!'

The music of another foreign country, though of much less value, also claimed his attention, at least for a few moments, on account of its unusual rhythm which he imitated in some of his piano music. It is the popular art of the United States. He wrote of it in the following amusing terms: 'At last! . . . the King of American music is within our walls! That is to say that during a whole week Mr. J. P. Sousa "and his band" will reveal to us the beauties of American music and how to use it in the best society. One must really be singularly gifted to conduct this music. Thus, Mr. Sousa beats time in circles, or he shakes an imaginary salad, or sweeps up imaginary dust, and catches a butterfly out of a contrabass-tuba. American music may be the only kind which can find a rhythm for unspeakable cake-walks. If so, I confess that at present this appears to be its sole claim to superiority over other music . . . and Mr. Sousa is indisputably its king.'

IX

The World of Music: audiences, interpreters, virtuosi and conductors, commentators and arrangers, critics.

THE title which Claude Debussy gave to a collection of his articles shows how little liking he had for musical audiences. He observed in amateurs as in critics a spirit of indifference that is hostile to music. Monsieur Croche's statement is explicit. When Debussy asks the phantom what his profession is, he replies 'Antidilettante', 'in a voice which silenced all comment', and the dry, downright old man utters his invective 'in an exasperated monotone: "Have you noticed the hostility of a concert audience? Have you studied those faces, grey with boredom, indifference or sheer stupidity? They never enter into the pure realm of drama expressed in the symphonic conflict where one may glimpse the possibility of reaching the pinnacle of music, there to breathe an atmosphere of perfect beauty. These people, sir, always look like more or less well-behaved guests. They patiently endure their boredom, and if they do not go away, it is because they must be seen at the end—else why should they have come? You will agree that it is enough to make one hate music for ever. . . ." Why does this dull collection of people, by courtesy called an audience, throng to the concert halls? Some of them are more interested in orchestral pantomime than in artistic feeling.' Others care only for the soloists: 'The attraction which the public feels for a virtuoso is not unlike that which draws a crowd to a circus. There is always the hope that something exciting will happen: Mr. Ysaÿe is going to play the violin with M. Colonne on his shoulders, or else, M. Pugno will, at the close of his piece, seize the piano between his teeth. . . .' In Paris at any rate, quite a number of music-lovers are drawn to the Concerts Colonne only by an absurd craze for foreign conductors. Then, too, there are the snobs, the Parisians of the Société des Grandes Auditions, for instance, or frequenters of Monte Carlo, 'delightful adventurers' and 'charming cosmopolitan young ladies'. This comparatively small class of audience—'for music is not really much loved in this wide world'—has also this defect that as a rule it likes only one kind of music. 'But to love only one form of it is really not to love it!' Debussy, more than any other musician, experienced the unpleasantness of the instinctive opposition of the musical public to new works. Though this sometimes saddened him, it never astonished him. 'I made music in order to serve music to the best of my ability and with no other thought. It was logical, therefore, that this music should run the risk of displeasing those who love only one kind of music and who remain jealously faithful to her in spite of her wrinkles and rouge.'

The audience, no matter what its composition, has the bad habit of applauding and of organizing 'the barbaric noise of hand clapping'. It is an unpleasing custom, 'a pristine instinct which had its origin in the Stone Age, to strike our hands one against the other and utter war-cries so as to demonstrate our most enthusiastic approval'. Such a noise is, he says, inadmissible: 'A true impression of beauty could produce no other effect than a desire for silence. . . . When you see the sunset—that daily scene of enchantment, does it ever occur to you to applaud?'

Monsieur Croche's enemies, the amateurs who constitute an ignorant, snobbish, and noisy audience, are put to varying and sometimes trying tests. All goes well as long as Beethoven is played: 'Here one is secure, being called upon only to admire, free to exchange knowing smiles at definite passages, always the same since they are passed on from generation to generation. . . . On leaving the hall one may say with assurance: "Beethoven! What a genius!" Besides, any other attitude would be merely a worse form of snobbery.' It is not such an easy matter on the days when one has to 'submit to that nerve-laden atmosphere which is a special characteristic of the Sunday concerts when a new composer is produced. In the first place, one has to form an opinion and that is not always easy. Is it better to appear to have understood, or should one's attitude be one of obdurate intolerance towards these novel harmonies? What a problem! Indeed, we often look at things without seeing them properly—witness the landscapes whose praises have not been sung. Imagination counts for so much in appreciation! In the matter of hearing, we are perhaps worse.'

But is it fair to condemn all audiences without distinction? No, for beside these odious amateurs, sincere lovers of music are to be found whose opinion is of more value even if they find it difficult to put it into words: 'We may be sure that there are very worthy people who only hear one bar in eight . . . this proportion is not fixed, it must indeed vary with each individual. It stands to reason, therefore, that at the end of a piece several bars are missing and their accounts do not work out right! It is not easy to admit this deficiency unless one resorts to the usual trick of remarking thoughtfully: "One would want to hear that several times." . . . That is absolutely false! When you hear music properly—specialized training and study apart—you hear right away what you should hear. The rest is only a matter of surroundings or external influence. An audience is never of itself hostile to music: often it does not even bother about the composer—a point specialists should bear in mind. But there are those terrible amateurs who do not come to amuse themselves; and we must be careful not to talk nonsense in front of them. You have to restrain yourself; and, like the child who is made to *choose* the very cake it did not like, you sulk inwardly. To tell the truth, it is no joke to be an audience! You can't help hoping they will set aside some Sundays for the study of the cup and ball game which calls for unusual skill but which, at any rate, demands no special aural gifts.'

Wagnerians are, needless to say, classed among the hostile amateurs. In a preceding chapter we have seen this Germanic group made a target for his keen-edged irony. With them are included those who profess contempt for Gounod: 'There are very clever people who by dint of hearing music every day and every type of music, come to consider themselves musicians. They never write music themselves . . . they merely encourage others. This is how a school is usually created. Do not mention Gounod to these: they would despise you from the heights of their gods. The most charming thing about these gods is that they are constantly changing. Fortunately the influence of these people on the public is *nil*, for the crowd 'in spite of many aesthetic efforts always return to the music they are accustomed to. It may not always be in the best taste. It fluctuates unaccountably between "Le Père la Victoire" and the "Walküre". That strange entity known as the "élite" can beat the drums in honour of names that are renowned or accepted—like hats, these vary according to the fashion. It is all in vain. The "élite" waste their breath. The great nameless heart of the crowd is not easily caught. Art continues to take its own course . . . the Opera goes on performing "Faust".'

These lines were written in 1906. Debussy is pessimistic in his analysis of the relations between art and the masses: 'One should nevertheless make up one's mind to admit that art is absolutely useless to the masses. Neither does it express the feelings of the "élite"—who are often more stupid than the masses. Art is beauty in all its strength, bursting forth when it must, with a fatal and secret force. But one cannot order the masses to love beauty any more than one can reasonably insist on their walking on their hands. It may be remarked in passing that the spontaneous influence of Berlioz on the masses is almost universal.'

In 1910 a critique on Italian music drew from him a remark that showed the same feeling of despondency: 'The public in general enjoys works that are in bad taste. There have been such works at all times. They supply a demand, and do what one will, they cannot be prevented.... If the public is sometimes weaned from them, it quickly returns.... Beautiful works will make themselves felt in their own way, the public has nothing to say to it for it does not understand.'

As early as 1903 Debussy had devoted almost an entire feuilleton in *Gil Blas* to the question of art for the people. It began with a good deal of mockery—indeed, there is bitterness beneath the bantering tone. He gives a list of the various attempts in this direction made in Paris: the 'Conservatoire de Mimi Pinson', whose aim is to broaden the outlook of young girls 'whose artistic ideals were hitherto bounded on the North by P. Delmet,[1] and on the South by Pierre Decourcelle'[2]; the 'Théâtre-roulotte' of Catulle Mendès and the 'Trente ans de Théâtre'. 'I have', says Debussy, 'personally assisted at efforts to propagate a taste for art among the people. I must confess that my recollection of them is most depressing.... Those who organize these undertakings generally assume an air of condescending goodwill which the unfortunate people

[1] See footnote to page 91.

[2] Pierre Decourcelle—dramatist and novelist, born in Paris, 1856. The best known of his plays is 'Les Deux Gosses'.

easily recognize as forced and studied. Certain it is that they always make up their minds to laugh or to cry to order, which is not altogether sincere. An instinctive feeling of envy hovers vaguely around this fleeting vision of luxury brought for a moment into all these dull lives. The women calculate the price of the dresses with a forced laugh; the men take stock . . . and dream impossible dreams. Others begrudge their ten sous, and all go sadly home to supper. The soup is not a success that night—it has a slightly salty taste of tears, believe me!'

Then comes an ironical satire on the organizers of popular entertainments, both fools and knaves: 'I quite realize the motive of these social ambitions, and far-seeing enthusiasms. It is undoubtedly stimulating to play at being a little Buddha, living on an egg and two glasses of water a day and giving the rest to the poor; dreaming interminable dreams of cosmogony, pantheism, the evolution of nature and voluptuous nebulosities of the ego, and the non-ego, reabsorbed in the universal soul. . . . It is all very fine, it sounds well in conversation; but unfortunately it is not in the least practical and can even bring about dangerous results.'

The type of performance to be given should be determined on. It is a mistake to adopt the custom of the popular theatre where the regular, traditional repertoire alternates with 'old worn-out dramas of the romantic period'. The form of theatrical art provided for the people should 'adapt itself to the majority, from the point of view both of mentality and of setting'. The popular theatre should not seek its repertoire among modern plays. These, with their psychological and social problems, are not suited to people who need distraction from their daily life and domestic worries. Their entertainment should rather be sought among the Greeks, in Euripides, Sophocles, Aeschylus, where 'the great human emotions are drawn in such simple lines and with such natural tragic effects that they are comprehensible to the least cultured and the least educated minds'.

The ancient theatrical formula might be employed: 'Let us return to tragedy and supplement its primitive musical setting with the infinite resources of the modern orchestra and a chorus of countless voices. We should bear in mind, too, the great variety of effects that may be obtained from Pantomime and Dancing by developing their interpretative possibilities to the utmost—that is to say, to the capacity of a crowd. In this connexion, valuable suggestions are to be found in the entertainments got up by Javanese princes. In these performances the seduction of that wordless language—pantomime—is irresistible, because action and not formula is the medium of expression. The unfortunate thing about our theatre is that we have limited it to the more obviously intelligible elements. The other mode of expression would be so beautiful that nothing else would satisfy us. It would be difficult of realization, no doubt.' In order to carry out this idea Debussy suggests that 'a loan be raised. It would be impossible to find a more worthy or more patriotic object for such a loan. . . . Scattered elements of goodwill must be brought together in an impulse of irresistible force which will ruthlessly sweep away those booths where the showman glibly invites the public to his sinister, empty performance.'

All this is not easy. Opera cannot be staged as can a play. There must be singers, a chorus, an orchestra. 'In a case of absolute necessity one can always provide an actor, as the old Théâtre-Libre has truly exemplified; but there are as yet no powers of suggestion potent enough to enable the first comer to play the double-bass. Although it may not appear so, this fact is extremely important! . . .'

The bourgeois audience at ordinary concerts often irritates Debussy. He fails to admire their sincerity and heaps vituperation on their snobbery. The musician reproaches them with not being able to distinguish between the artist and the mummer. He would like to see more appreciation for those interpreters who are content to give a simple and musical performance and who do not unduly superimpose their personality on that of the composer in order to impress the crowd and win applause. His portrayal of translators or interpreters of music, such as conductors, is faithful and lifelike.

In an account of a concert given at the Schola he draws a very realistic picture of the orchestra pupils endeavouring to realize 'the desire for perfection demanded of them by Vincent d'Indy, with his engaging smile. His very gesture as he beats time seems an embrace enfolding these youthful minds.' In his first article, in 1901, he thanks Chevillard for refraining from the toreador-like pantomime which certain international conductors affect. 'This fashion of sticking banderillas in the head of an English horn, or striking terror into unfortunate trombones with the gesture of a matador, was very disconcerting. M. Chevillard is satisfied if his audience is convinced that he understands very well: it is so simple, but so difficult to achieve.'

At the time of the performances of 'Parsifal' in 1903, Alfred Cortot, who conducted them, is ridiculed for imitating too closely his colleagues beyond the Rhine: 'M. Cortot, more than any other French conductor, has adopted the pantomime customary with German conductors. He affects the Nikisch lock of hair (the latter is Hungarian, by the way), and the excited movements which agitate this lock of hair at every nuance are fascinating in the extreme.... Notice its sad and weary droop in soft passages, intercepting all communication between M. Cortot and the audience. . . . Then see it proudly rise in warlike passages . . . as M. Cortot advances on the orchestra pointing a menacing baton as do the banderilleros to disconcert the bull . . . (the orchestra remain as cool as Greenlanders—they've seen worse before). Like Weingartner he bends affectionately over the first violins, whispering intimate confidences; then he turns to the trombones to remonstrate with them in a gesture which would seem to say: "Come, my children, courage! Be trombones and forget yourselves." And the docile trombones immediately swallow their slides.' But he makes kindly allowance for the young conductor: 'It is but fair to add that M. Cortot knows Wagner inside out and that he is a perfect musician. He is young, his love for music is very disinterested—these are reasons enough for not blaming him too severely for gestures that are more decorative than useful.'

The exuberant pantomime of the 'international conductors' does not prevent him from paying tribute to their good qualities. When Arthur Nikisch came to Paris with the Berlin Philharmonic Orchestra in the spring of 1901, Debussy gave him both praise and blame: 'M. Nikisch is distinguished for his attitude and his lock of hair. To these, fortunately, are added more important assets, and his orchestra is marvellously disciplined. M. Nikisch is an incomparable virtuoso; it would almost seem that his virtuosity makes him forget what is due to good taste! I shall take an instance from his performance of the overture to "Tannhäuser", in which he exacts from the trombones a volume of sound altogether worthy of the stout lady cast for the sentimental roles at the Casino of Suresnes. Then, too, he brings out the horns in places where there is no special reason for stressing them. There is no excuse for these effects; and they surprise one in a finished musician such as M. Nikisch shows himself to be in every other particular. He had previously given proof of the high quality of his gifts in "Till Eulenspiegel" by Richard Strauss. . . . M. Nikisch conducted this tumultuous music with amazing sang-froid and the ovation which greeted him and his orchestra was more than justified.'

In 1903 he rather made fun of Weingartner for

his treatment of the Pastoral Symphony, performed 'with the care of a meticulous gardener'. He is sketched thus: 'At first sight M. Weingartner's appearance suggests a new knife. His gestures are almost rectilinear in their elegance: then suddenly his arms make merciless signs that draw wails from the trombones and send the cymbals crazy.... It is very effective—almost miraculous, indeed, and the audience hardly knows how to express its enthusiasm.'

Richard Strauss is represented as a conqueror, a dominating figure whom few resist: 'M. Strauss does not affect a crazy lock of hair, neither has he the gestures of an epileptic. He is tall, with the frank, resolute mien of great explorers who encounter savage tribes with a smile on their lips. This attitude is perhaps necessary to shake the audience out of its polite indifference? His forehead, however, is that of a musician, whilst the eyes and the gestures are those of a superman, as described by Nietzsche who must have inspired his energy....'

Debussy had seen Hans Richter conduct the 'Ring' in London in 1903. He wrote of him almost with veneration: 'Doctor Richter conducted its first performance at Bayreuth in 1876. At that time his hair and beard were light red. His hair has thinned since then, but the eyes behind his gold-rimmed spectacles have retained their wonderful brilliance.... The eyes of a prophet, for such he is indeed, and such he would remain, in so far as the Wagnerian cult is concerned, were it not for Mme Cosima Wagner's decision to replace him by her estimable and mediocre son, Siegfried Wagner.... Richter resembles a prophet, but when he conducts the orchestra, he is the Almighty . . . (and indeed the Almighty Himself would hardly undertake this task without first seeking counsel with Richter). Whilst his right hand, armed with a small, unpretentious baton, assures precision of rhythm, his left hand multiplies itself, indicating to all what they must do. This hand is undulating and versatile and incredibly supple. Then, just when one is convinced that it would be impossible to produce greater wealth of sound, both arms are raised at once. The orchestra leaps through the music with an irresistible ardour, and the most rooted indifference is swept away like a wisp of straw. These gestures are always discreet, they never offend the eye or interpose themselves between the music and the audience.'

Debussy willingly praises virtuosi, like Ysaÿe, Pugno, and others whom he had occasion to mention. But he is merciless in his criticism of certain persons who endeavour to render music in terms of literature or otherwise treat masterpieces without due respect: 'commentators, adaptors, meddlers . . . that countless horde that exists only for the purpose of wrapping unfortunate masterpieces in a fog of words and high-sounding epithets. Berlioz is not their only victim, alas! There is the famous Mona Lisa smile which has been for ever labelled as "mysterious". . . . Beethoven's Choral Symphony which lent itself to such superhuman interpretations that for a long time this clear, powerful work was turned into a bogy for the public. Wagner's entire work too which, thanks to its own solidity, resisted the industrious ardour of his annotators. All these efforts represent a special kind of literature—indeed, a regular profession which has infinite possibilities provided one keeps within its limits; for the task of speaking of others inevitably precludes that of speaking of oneself—which is sometimes a dangerous undertaking. In some respects this is praiseworthy. On the other hand, it is perhaps the result of insufficient knowledge which is more or less apparent according to the skill employed.'

There is another class of musicians that Debussy does not spare, these are the critics. Their articles appear to him to breathe a hatred of music. It is true that he himself was among the most discussed and the least understood of composers. In the course of a conversation with a journalist, on the day following the production of 'Pelléas et Mélisande', he even considered it necessary to defend himself against certain critics of his masterpiece. Later on, when he was composing the 'Martyre de Saint Sébastien', and much to his regret was obliged to improvise the music hastily, he learnt how real and how intense was the hostility directed against his 'childish musical grammar', which shocked 'those who favour deceit and artifice'. 'I am glad of it,' he added, 'I shall do nothing to create adversaries, but neither shall I do anything to turn enmities to friendships. I must endeavour to be a great artist so that I may dare to be myself and suffer for my faith. Those who feel as I do will but love me the more. The others will avoid me, hate me. I shall make no effort to conciliate them.'

His conclusion, which will serve as a final word for this book, made up of his own theories, is stamped with a spiritual scepticism: 'On that distant day—I trust it is still very far off—when I shall no longer be a subject for dispute, I shall indeed have cause for bitter self-reproach. For in those last works, that odious hypocrisy which will enable me to please all mankind will have prevailed.'

LIST OF CLAUDE DEBUSSY'S ARTICLES

In 1914 Claude Debussy collected some of his musical criticisms with slight alterations and additions. The greater number of the articles that appeared in the *Revue Blanche* (1901), about half the feuilletons from *Gil Blas* (1903), and an article from *Musica* (1905) were to make up a collection entitled 'Monsieur Croche, antidilettante' which was to have appeared towards the end of 1914.

The book was in the printers' hands when the war broke out. Owing to the invasion of Belgium, this work was interrupted and was only continued after a delay of seven years. Owing to this delay, the collection has unfortunately become a posthumous work, as is pointed out in a note by the editor. 'Monsieur Croche, antidilettante' is one of the volumes of the collection of the 'Bibliophiles fantaisistes' (published in Paris by Dorbon aîné, 1921, five hundred and fifty copies). An English translation of it appeared in 1927 (London, Noel Douglas).

Our quotations are taken from Debussy's original articles, and not from the 'Monsieur Croche' arrangement.

In the following list the extracts from articles which make up the volume 'Monsieur Croche, antidilettante' are indicated by the abbreviation *Cr.* after each title and a number in roman figures corresponding to the numbers of the twenty-five chapters of the collection made by Debussy.

I. *REVUE BLANCHE*

1 *April* 1901. Music (*Cr.* I).—Au Concert Colonne: le *Faust* de Schumann.—Au Concert Lamoureux: Ouverture pour le *Roi Lear* d'A. Savard, 1re audition; le troisième acte de *Siegfried*.—Société Nationale: Concert d'orchestre du 16 mars: *Symphonie* de Witkowski (*Cr.* III), *Poèmes danois* de Delius.

15 *April* 1901. La Chambre d'enfants de M. Moussorgsky (*Cr.* IV).—Une sonate pour piano de Paul Dukas (*Cr.* V).—Concerts symphoniques du Vaudeville: German conductors (*Cr.* VI).

1 *May* 1901. Good Friday: Bach (*Cr.* VI).—La Neuvième Symphonie (*Cr.* III).

15 *May* 1901. Opéras (*Cr.* VII).—*Le Roi de Paris* de George Hüe.—L'*Ouragan* d'Alfred Bruneau.

1 *June* 1901. Concerts Nikisch (*Cr.* VIII).—La Musique en plein air (*Cr.* X).—Concerts.

1 *July* 1901. L'entretien avec M. Croche (*Cr.* I).

15 *November* 1901. De quelques superstitions et d'un opéra: Monsieur Croche et les *Barbares* de Saint-Saëns (*Cr.* II).

1 *December* 1901. D'*Ève* à *Grisélidis*, Massenet (*Cr.* IX).

II. *GIL BLAS*

12 *January* 1903. L'*Étranger* de V. d'Indy au théâtre de la Monnaie (*Cr.* XXI).

19 *January* 1903. Considérations sur la musique de plein air (*Cr.* X).—Les Concerts: *Namouna* de Lalo, la *Damnation de Faust*, prélude du deuxième acte de l'*Étranger*, Concerto de piano de Léon Moreau.—Le Prince F. de Bavière.

21 *and* 26 *January* 1903. *Titania* de Georges Hüe (*Cr.* XI).

2 *February* 1903. *Castor et Pollux* de Rameau à la Schola (*Cr.* XII).

16 *February* 1903. F. Weingartner: *Symphonie pastorale*, *Mazeppa* (*Cr.* XIII).—Reprise de la *Traviata* à l'Opéra-Comique.

23 *February* 1903. Lettre ouverte à M. le Chevalier C. W. Gluck (*Cr.* XXV).—A la Société Nationale: *Symphonie* pour orgue de Vierne, *Quelques danses* de Chausson.—Au Concert Lamoureux: *Symphonie* de Guy Ropartz.

2 *March* 1903. Pour le peuple(*Cr.* XIV).—Siegfried Wagner au Concert Lamoureux (*Cr.* XVII).

9 *March* 1903. De l'Opéra et de ses rapports avec la musique. —A la Société Nationale: *Symphonie* de Wailly, *Ballade* de Fauré, Variations de Rhené-Baton. Mort d'Albert Cahen.

16 *March* 1903. Au Concert Colonne: M. Saint-Saëns (*Cr.* II): *Parysatis*.—Alfred Bachelet.—Concerts Lamoureux: *Antar*, *Concerto* de Grieg.

19 *March* 1903. *Muguette* d'Edmond Missa à l'Opéra-Comique.

23 *March* 1903. *Les Huguenots.*—A propos de *Muguette.*—Au Concert Lamoureux: *Réformation-Symphonie* de Mendelssohn, Émile Sauer, *Penthésilée* d'Alfred Bruneau, *Danse Macabre* de Saint-Saëns.

30 *March* 1903. Le Mozart de Saint-Maur.—A la Société Nationale: *Suite* pour piano de Samazeuilh, *Serres chaudes* de Chausson, *Variations* de Dukas.—Richard Strauss (*Cr.* XV).—Au Concert Colonne.

6 *April* 1903. *Parsifal* et la Société des Grandes Auditions de France (*Cr.* XVI).—Centenaire de l'Académie de France à Rome.—Les Concerts.

13 *April* 1903. L'*Or du Rhin* au concert.—Les *Béatitudes* de César Franck (*Cr.* XVIII).—Scarlatti (*Cr.* XIX).—J. de Reszké.

20 *April* 1903.—Edvard-Hagerup Grieg (*Cr.* XX).—J. P. Sousa and his band.

27 *April* 1903. Une renaissance de l'Opéra-bouffe (*le Sire de Vergy* de Cl. Terrasse).—Reprise de *Werther.*

5 *May* 1903. La *Tétralogie* de Wagner à Londres (*Cr.* XXII).

8 *May* 1903. Berlioz et M. Gunsbourg (*Cr.* XXIII).

19 *May* 1903. *Henry VIII* de Saint-Saëns.

1 *June* 1903. Impressions sur la *Tétralogie* à Londres.

6 *June* 1903. *La Petite Maison* de W. Chaumet.

10 *June* 1903. Les Impressions d'un Prix de Rome (*Cr.* II).

28 *June* 1903. Le bilan musical en 1903: Opéra, Opéra-Comique, Opéras étrangers.

III. *MUSICA*

October 1902. Sur l'Orientation musicale.

May 1903. Considérations sur le Prix de Rome au point de vue musical (*Cr.* II).

July 1906. A propos de Charles Gounod (*Cr.* XXIV).

January 1908. Mary Garden.

March 1911. Les rapports du vers et de la musique.

IV. *MERCURE DE FRANCE*

January 1903. Réponse à l'enquête sur l'influence allemande (interview).

V. *REVUE BLEUE*

2 *April* 1904. Réponse à l'enquête sur l'état actuel de la musique française (interview).

VI. *LE FIGARO*

16 *May* 1902. *Pelléas* et la critique (interview).
8 *May* 1908. A propos d'*Hippolyte et Aricie*.
14 *February* 1909. Que faire au Conservatoire? (interview).

VII. *COMŒDIA*

4 *November* 1909. La musique d'aujourd'hui et de demain (interview).
31 *January* 1910. La musique moderne italienne (interview).
17 *December* 1910. Interview.
26 *January* 1911. Décentralisation musicale (interview).
18 *May* 1911. *Saint Sébastien* (interview).
1 *February* 1914. *La Boîte à Joujoux* et *Fêtes Galantes* (interview).

VIII. *PARIS-JOURNAL*

20 *May* 1910. Une renaissance de l'idéal classique (interview).

IX. *LE GAULOIS*

10 *January* 1911. La musique étrangère et les compositeurs français (interview).

X. *EXCELSIOR*

9 *March* 1911. La musique russe et les compositeurs français.
11 *February* 1911. Le *Martyre de Saint Sébastien* (interview).
15 *September* 1913. L'opéra de demain (contribution to a symposium).

XI. *VARIOUS*

February 1908. L'*Influence de Wagner*.
16 *October* 1910. Le Festival français de Munich.
8 *January* 1911. Debussy jugé par lui-même.

22 *January* 1911. La Musique.

15 *May* 1911. Le *Martyre de Saint Sébastien.*

January 1914. Interview with M. D. Calvocoressi, 'The Étude'. Philadelphia.

XII. *MONTHLY S.I.M.*

November 1912. Crise de la musique française.—Concerts Colonne: *Symphonie pastorale*, *Symphonie fantastique*, Impressions d'Italie de G. Charpentier.

December 1912. Du respect dans l'art.—Concerts Colonne: *De l'ombre à la lumière* de Paul Pierné; *Mort et Transfiguration* de Richard Strauss; Festival Beethoven.

15 *January* 1913. Fin d'année.—Concerts Colonne: *Poème* de Chausson, *A Marie endormie* de Guy Ropartz, concerto de Bach pour violon.

15 *February* 1913. Du goût—Notes sur les Concerts Colonne.

15 *March* 1913. Du précurseur: Wilhelm Rust.—Concerts Colonne: Fanelli.

15 *May* 1913. État musical actuel.—Concert du Théâtre des Champs-Élysées.

November 1913. Musique et nature; état musical. Notes sur les Concerts Colonne et des Champs-Élysées.

December 1913. Musique espagnole.—Concerts Colonne: *Faust et Hélène* de Lili Boulanger.

January 1914. Lettre de Russie.

February 1914. Sur deux chefs-d'œuvre: *Parsifal.*—Concerts: L'*Étranger* de Max d'Ollone.

March 1914. Pour la musique.—Concerts Colonne: *La Vengeance des Fleurs* de Grovlez, 3e *Symphonie* de Gédalge.

XIII. *PRÉFACE D'UNE ÉDITION DE CHOPIN*

1915. Preface and notes for the works of Chopin (Édition classique Durand, Paris).

XIV. *LETTRE-PRÉFACE*

December 1916. 'Lettre-préface', to Paul Huvelin, of the *Pour la Musique française*, a collection of lectures by various authors (Paris, Crès, 1916).

INDEX OF PERSONS

Index of Persons

Index of Persons

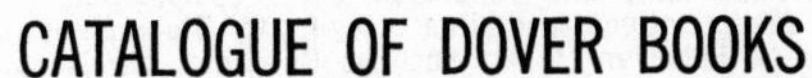

CATALOGUE OF DOVER BOOKS

Music

A GENERAL HISTORY OF MUSIC, Charles Burney. A detailed coverage of music from the Greeks up to 1789, with full information on all types of music: sacred and secular, vocal and instrumental, operatic and symphonic. Theory, notation, forms, instruments, innovators, composers, performers, typical and important works, and much more in an easy, entertaining style. Burney covered much of Europe and spoke with hundreds of authorities and composers so that this work is more than a compilation of records . . . it is a living work of careful and first-hand scholarship. Its account of thoroughbass (18th century) Italian music is probably still the best introduction on the subject. A recent NEW YORK TIMES review said, "Surprisingly few of Burney's statements have been invalidated by modern research . . . still of great value." Edited and corrected by Frank Mercer. 35 figures. Indices. 1915pp. 5⅜ x 8. 2 volumes. T36 The Set, Clothbound **$12.50**

A DICTIONARY OF HYMNOLOGY, John Julian. This exhaustive and scholarly work has become known as an invaluable source of hundreds of thousands of important and often difficult to obtain facts on the history and use of hymns in the western world. Everyone interested in hymns will be fascinated by the accounts of famous hymns and hymn writers and amazed by the amount of practical information he will find. More than 30,000 entries on individual hymns, giving authorship, date and circumstances of composition, publication, textual variations, translations, denominational and ritual usage, etc. Biographies of more than 9,000 hymn writers, and essays on important topics such as Christmas carols and children's hymns, and much other unusual and valuable information. A 200 page double-columned index of first lines — the largest in print. Total of 1786 pages in two reinforced clothbound volumes. 6¼ x 9¼. The set, T333 Clothbound **$17.50**

MUSIC IN MEDIEVAL BRITAIN, F. Ll. Harrison. The most thorough, up-to-date, and accurate treatment of the subject ever published, beautifully illustrated. Complete account of institutions and choirs; carols, masses, and motets; liturgy and plainsong; and polyphonic music from the Norman Conquest to the Reformation. Discusses the various schools of music and their reciprocal influences; the origin and development of new ritual forms; development and use of instruments; and new evidence on many problems of the period. Reproductions of scores, over 200 excerpts from medieval melodies. Rules of harmony and dissonance; influence of Continental styles; great composers (Dunstable, Cornysh, Fairfax, etc.); and much more. Register and index of more than 400 musicians. Index of titles. General Index. 225-item bibliography. 6 Appendices. xix + 491pp. 5⅝ x 8¾. T705 Clothbound **$10.00**

THE MUSIC OF SPAIN, Gilbert Chase. Only book in English to give concise, comprehensive account of Iberian music; new Chapter covers music since 1941. Victoria, Albéniz, Cabezón, Pedrell, Turina, hundreds of other composers; popular and folk music; the Gypsies; the guitar; dance, theatre, opera, with only extensive discussion in English of the Zarzuela; virtuosi such as Casals; much more. "Distinguished . . . readable," Saturday Review. 400-item bibliography. Index. 27 photos. 383pp. 5⅜ x 8. T549 Paperbound **$2.25**

ON STUDYING SINGING, Sergius Kagen. An intelligent method of voice-training, which leads you around pitfalls that waste your time, money, and effort. Exposes rigid, mechanical systems, baseless theories, deleterious exercises. "Logical, clear, convincing . . . dead right," Virgil Thomson, N.Y. Herald Tribune. "I recommend this volume highly," Maggie Teyte, Saturday Review. 119pp. 5⅜ x 8. T622 Paperbound **$1.35**

WILLIAM LAWES, M. Lefkowitz. This is the definitive work on Lawes, the versatile, prolific, and highly original "King's musician" of 17th century England. His life is reconstructed from original documents, and nearly every piece he ever wrote is examined and evaluated: his fantasias, pavans, violin "sonatas," lyra viol and bass viol suites, and music for harp and theorbo; and his songs, masques, and theater music to words by Herrick ("Gather Ye Rosebuds"), Jonson, Suckling, Shirley, and others. The author shows the innovations of dissonance, augmented triad, and other Italian influences Lawes helped introduce to England. List of Lawes' complete works and several complete scores by this major precursor of Purcell and the 18th century developments. Index. 5 Appendices. 52 musical excerpts, many never before in print. Bibliography. x + 320pp. 5⅜ x 8. T706 Clothbound **$10.00**

THE FUGUE IN BEETHOVEN'S PIANO MUSIC, J. V. Cockshoot. The first study of a neglected aspect of Beethoven's genius: his ability as a writer of fugues. Analyses of early studies and published works demonstrate his original and powerful contributions to composition. 34 works are examined, with 143 musical excerpts. For all pianists, teachers, students, and music-minded readers with a serious interest in Beethoven. Index. 93-item bibliography. Illustration of original score for "Fugue in C." xv + 212pp. 5⅝ x 8⅜. T704 Clothbound **$6.00**

JOHANN SEBASTIAN BACH, Philipp Spitta. The complete and unabridged text of the definitive study of Bach. Written some 70 years ago, it is still unsurpassed for its coverage of nearly all aspects of Bach's life and work. There could hardly be a finer non-technical introduction to Bach's music than the detailed, lucid analyses which Spitta provides for hundreds of individual pieces. 26 solid pages are devoted to the B minor mass, for example, and 30 pages to the glorious St. Matthew Passion. This monumental set also includes a major analysis of the music of the 18th century: Buxtehude, Pachelbel, etc. "Unchallenged as the last word on one of the supreme geniuses of music," John Barkham, SATURDAY REVIEW SYNDICATE. Total of 1819pp. 2 volumes. Heavy cloth binding. 5⅜ x 8. T252 The set, Clothbound **$13.50**

THE LIFE OF MOZART, O. Jahn. Probably the largest amount of material on Mozart's life and works ever gathered together in one book! Its 1350 authoritative and readable pages cover every event in his life, and contain a full critique of almost every piece he ever wrote, including sketches and intimate works. There is a full historical-cultural background, and vast research into musical and literary history, sources of librettos, prior treatments of Don Juan legend, etc. This is the complete and unaltered text of the definitive Townsend translation, with foreword by Grove. 5 engraved portraits from Salzburg archives. 4 facsimiles in Mozart's hand. 226 musical examples. 4 Appendixes, including complete list of Mozart's compositions, with Köchel numbers (fragmentary works included). Total of xxviii + 1352pp. Three volume set. 5⅜ x 8.
T85 Vol. I Clothbound **$5.00**
T86 Vol. II Clothbound **$5.00**
The set **$10.00**

BEETHOVEN'S QUARTETS, J. de Marliave. The most complete and authoritative study ever written, enjoyable for scholar and layman alike. The 16 quartets and Grand Fugue are all analyzed bar by bar and theme by theme, not over-technically, but concentrating on mood and effects. Complete background material for each composition: influences, first reviews, etc. Preface by Gabriel Fauré. Introduction and notes by J. Escarra. Translated by Hilda Andrews. 321 musical examples. xxiii + 379pp. 5⅜ x 8. T694 Paperbound **$2.00**

STRUCTURAL HEARING: TONAL COHERENCE IN MUSIC, Felix Salzer. Written by a pupil of the late Heinrich Schenker, this is not only the most thorough exposition in English of the Schenker method but also extends the Schenker approach to include modern music, the middle ages, and renaissance music. It explores the phenomenon of tonal organization by means of a detailed analysis and discussion of more than 500 musical pieces. It casts new light for the reader acquainted with harmony upon the understanding of musical compositions, problems of musical coherence, and connection between theory and composition. "Has been the foundation on which all teaching in music theory has been based at this college," Leopold Mannes, President of The Mannes College of Music. 2 volumes. Total of 658pp. 6½ x 9¼.
The set, T418 Clothbound **$8.00**

ANTONIO STRADIVARI: HIS LIFE AND WORK (1644-1737), W. Henry Hill, Arthur F. Hill, and Alfred E. Hill. Still the only book that really delves into life and art of the incomparable Italian craftsman, maker of the finest musical instruments in the world today. The authors, expert violin-makers themselves, discuss Stradivari's ancestry, his construction and finishing techniques, distinguished characteristics of many of his instruments and their locations. Included, too, is story of introduction of his instruments into France, England, first revelation of their supreme merit, and information on his labels, number of instruments made, prices, mystery of ingredients of his varnish, tone of pre-1684 Stradivari violin and changes between 1684 and 1690. An extremely interesting, informative account for all music lovers, from craftsman to concert-goer. Republication of original (1902) edition. New introduction by Sydney Beck, Head of Rare Book and Manuscript Collections, Music Division, New York Public Library. Analytical index by Rembert Wurlitzer. Appendixes. 68 illustrations. 30 full-page plates. 4 in color. xxvi + 315pp. 5⅜ x 8½. T425 Paperbound **$2.25**

THREE CLASSICS IN THE AESTHETIC OF MUSIC, Claude Debussy, Ferrucio Busoni, and Charles Ives. Three very different points of view by three top-ranking modern composers. "M. Croche, the Dilettante-Hater" consists of twenty-five brief articles written by Debussy between the years 1901 and 1905, a sparkling collection of personal commentary on a wide range of topics. Busoni's "Toward a New Aesthetic of Music" considers the nature of absolute music in an attempt to suggest answers to the question, What are the aims of music?, and discusses modern systems of tonality and harmony, the concept of unity of keys, etc. Ives's "Essays Before a Sonata," a literary complement to the movements of the author's "Concord, 1845" piano sonata, contains his most mature analysis of his art. Stimulating reading for musicians, music lovers, and philosophers of the arts. iv + 188pp. 5⅜ x 8½.
T320 Paperbound **$1.50**

Dover Classical Records

Now available directly to the public exclusively from Dover: top-quality recordings of fine classical music for only $2 per record! Originally released by a major company (except for the previously unreleased Gimpel recording of Bach) to sell for $5 and $6, these records were issued under our imprint only after they had passed a severe critical test. We insisted upon:

First-rate music that is enjoyable, musically important and culturally significant.

First-rate performances, where the artists have carried out the composer's intentions, in which the music is alive, vigorous, played with understanding and sympathy.

First-rate sound—clear, sonorous, fully balanced, crackle-free, whir-free.

Have in your home music by major composers, performed by such gifted musicians as Elsner, Gitlis, Wührer, the Barchet Quartet, Gimpel. Enthusiastically received when first released, many of these performances are definitive. The records are not seconds or remainders, but brand new pressings made on pure vinyl from carefully chosen master tapes. "All purpose" 12" monaural 33⅓ rpm records, they play equally well on hi-fi and stereo equipment. Fine music for discriminating music lovers, superlatively played, flawlessly recorded: there is no better way to build your library of recorded classical music at remarkable savings. There are no strings; this is not a come-on, not a club, forcing you to buy records you may not want in order to get a few at a lower price. Buy whatever records you want in any quantity, and never pay more than $2 each. Your obligation ends with your first purchase. And that's when ours begins. Dover's money-back guarantee allows you to return any record for any reason, even if you don't like the music, for a full, immediate refund, no questions asked.

MOZART: STRING QUARTET IN A MAJOR (K.464); STRING QUARTET IN C MAJOR ("DISSONANT", K.465), Barchet Quartet. The final two of the famed Haydn Quartets, high-points in the history of music. The A Major was accepted with delight by Mozart's contemporaries, but the C Major, with its dissonant opening, aroused strong protest. Today, of course, the remarkable resolutions of the dissonances are recognized as major musical achievements. "Beautiful warm playing," MUSICAL AMERICA. "Two of Mozart's loveliest quartets in a distinguished performance," REV. OF RECORDED MUSIC. (Playing time 58 mins.) HCR 5200 **$2.00**

MOZART: QUARTETS IN G MAJOR (K.80); D MAJOR (K.155); G MAJOR (K.156); C MAJOR (K157), Barchet Quartet. The early chamber music of Mozart receives unfortunately little attention. First-rate music of the Italian school, it contains all the lightness and charm that belongs only to the youthful Mozart. This is currently the only separate source for the composer's work of this time period. "Excellent," HIGH FIDELITY. "Filled with sunshine and youthful joy; played with verve, recorded sound live and brilliant," CHRISTIAN SCI. MONITOR. (Playing time 51 mins.) HCR 5201 **$2.00**

MOZART: SERENADE #9 IN D MAJOR ("POSTHORN", K.320); SERENADE #6 IN D MAJOR ("SERENATA NOTTURNA", K.239), Pro Musica Orch. of Stuttgart, under Edouard van Remoortel. For Mozart, the serenade was a highly effective form, since he could bring to it the immediacy and intimacy of chamber music as well as the free fantasy of larger group music. Both these serenades are distinguished by a playful, mischievous quality, a spirit perfectly captured in this fine performance. "A triumph, polished playing from the orchestra," HI FI MUSIC AT HOME. "Sound is rich and resonant, fidelity is wonderful," REV. OF RECORDED MUSIC. (Playing time 51 mins.) HCR 5202 **$2.00**

MOZART: DIVERTIMENTO IN E FLAT MAJOR FOR STRING TRIO (K.563); ADAGIO AND FUGUE IN F MINOR FOR STRING TRIO (K.404a), Kehr Trio. The Divertimento is one of Mozart's most beloved pieces, called by Einstein "the finest, most perfect trio ever heard." It is difficult to imagine a music lover who will not be delighted by it. This is the only recording of the lesser known Adagio and Fugue, written in 1782 and influenced by Bach's Well-Tempered Clavichord. "Extremely beautiful recording, strongly recommended," THE OBSERVER. "Superior to rival editions," HIGH FIDELITY. (Playing time 51 mins.) HCR 5203 **$2.00**

SCHUMANN: KREISLERIANA (OP.16); FANTASY IN C MAJOR ("FANTASIE," OP.17), Vlado Perlemuter, Piano. The vigorous Romantic imagination and the remarkable emotional qualities of Schumann's piano music raise it to special eminence in 19th century creativity. Both these pieces are rooted to the composer's tortuous romance with his future wife, Clara, and both receive brilliant treatment at the hands of Vlado Perlemuter, Paris Conservatory, proclaimed by Alfred Cortot "not only a great virtuoso but also a great musician." "The best Kreisleriana to date," BILLBOARD. (Playing time 55 mins.) HCR 5204 **$2.00**

SCHUMANN: TRIO #1, D MINOR; TRIO #3, G MINOR, Trio di Bolzano. The fiery, romantic, melodic Trio #1, and the dramatic, seldom heard Trio #3 are both movingly played by a fine chamber ensemble. No one personified Romanticism to the general public of the 1840's more than did Robert Schumann, and among his most romantic works are these trios for cello, violin and piano. "Ensemble and overall interpretation leave little to be desired," HIGH FIDELITY. "An especially understanding performance," REV. OF RECORDED MUSIC. (Playing time 54 mins.) HCR 5205 **$2.00**

SCHUMANN: TRIOS #1 IN D MINOR (OPUS 63) AND #3 IN G MINOR (OPUS 110), Trio di Bolzano. The fiery, romantic, melodic Trio #1 and the dramatic, seldom heard Trio #3 are both movingly played by a fine chamber ensemble. No one personified Romanticism to the general public of the 1840's more than did Robert Schumann, and among his most romantic works are these trios for cello, violin and piano. "Ensemble and overall interpretation leave little to be desired," HIGH FIDELITY. "An especially understanding performance," REV. OF RECORDED MUSIC. (Playing time 54 mins.) HCR 5205 **$2.00**

SCHUBERT: QUINTET IN A ("TROUT") (OPUS 114), AND NOCTURNE IN E FLAT (OPUS 148), Friedrich Wührer, Piano and Barchet Quartet. If there is a single piece of chamber music that is a universal favorite, it is probably Schubert's "Trout" Quintet. Delightful melody, harmonic resources, musical exuberance are its characteristics. The Nocturne (played by Wührer, Barchet, and Reimann) is an exquisite piece with a deceptively simple theme and harmony. "The best Trout on the market—Wührer is a fine Viennese-style Schubertian, and his spirit infects the Barchets," ATLANTIC MONTHLY. "Exquisitely recorded," ETUDE. (Playing time 44 mins.) HCR 5206 **$2.00**

SCHUBERT: PIANO SONATAS IN C MINOR AND B (OPUS 147), Friedrich Wührer. Schubert's sonatas retain the structure of the classical form, but delight listeners with romantic freedom and a special melodic richness. The C Minor, one of the Three Grand Sonatas, is a product of the composer's maturity. The B Major was not published until 15 years after his death. "Remarkable interpretation, reproduction of the first rank," DISQUES. "A superb pianist for music like this, musicianship, sweep, power, and an ability to integrate Schubert's measures such as few pianists have had since Schnabel," Harold Schonberg. (Playing time 49 mins.) HCR 5207 **$2.00**

STRAVINSKY: VIOLIN CONCERTO IN D, Ivry Gitlis, Cologne Orchestra; DUO CONCERTANTE, Ivry Gitlis, Violin, Charlotte Zelka, Piano, Cologne Orchestra; JEU DE CARTES, Bamberg Symphony, under Hollreiser. Igor Stravinsky is probably the most important composer of this century, and these three works are among the most significant of his neoclassical period of the 30's. The Violin Concerto is one of the few modern classics. Jeu de Cartes, a ballet score, bubbles with gaiety, color and melodiousness. "Imaginatively played and beautifully recorded," E. T. Canby, HARPERS MAGAZINE. "Gitlis is excellent, Hollreiser beautifully worked out," HIGH FIDELITY. (Playing time 55 mins.) HCR 5208 **$2.00**

GEMINIANI: SIX CONCERTI GROSSI, OPUS 3, Helma Elsner, Harpsichord, Barchet Quartet, Pro Musica Orch. of Stuttgart, under Reinhardt. Francesco Geminiani (1687-1762) has been rediscovered in the same musical exploration that revealed Scarlatti, Vivaldi, and Corelli. In form he is more sophisticated than the earlier Italians, but his music delights modern listeners with its combination of contrapuntal techniques and the full harmonies and rich melodies charcteristic of Italian music. This is the only recording of the six 1733 concerti: D Major, B Flat Minor, E Minor, G Minor, E Minor (bis), and D Minor. "I warmly recommend it, spacious, magnificent, I enjoyed every bar," C. Cudworth, RECORD NEWS. "Works of real charm, recorded with understanding and style," ETUDE. (Playing time 52 mins.) HCR 5209 **$2.00**

MODERN PIANO SONATAS: BARTOK: SONATA FOR PIANO; BLOCH: SONATA FOR PIANO (1935); PROKOFIEV, PIANO SONATA #7 IN B FLAT ("STALINGRAD"); STRAVINSKY: PIANO SONATA (1924), István Nádas, Piano. Shows some of the major forces and directions in modern piano music: Stravinsky's crisp austerity; Bartok's fusion of Hungarian folk motives; incisive diverse rhythms, and driving power; Bloch's distinctive emotional vigor; Prokofiev's brilliance and melodic beauty couched in pre-Romantic forms. "A most interesting documentation of the contemporary piano sonata. Nadas is a very good pianist." HIGH FIDELITY. (Playing time 59 mins.) HCR 5215 **$2.00**

VIVALDI: CONCERTI FOR FLUTE, VIOLIN, BASSOON, AND HARPSICHORD: #8 IN G MINOR, #21 IN F, #27 IN D, #7 IN D; SONATA #1 IN A MINOR, Gastone Tassinari, Renato Giangrandi, Giorgio Semprini, Arlette Eggmann. More than any other Baroque composer, Vivaldi moved the concerto grosso closer to the solo concert we deem standard today. In these concerti he wrote virtuosi music for the solo instruments, allowing each to introduce new material or expand on musical ideas, creating tone colors unusual even for Vivaldi. As a result, this record displays a new area of his genius, offering some of his most brilliant music. Performed by a top-rank European group. (Playing time 45 mins.) HCR 5216 **$2.00**

LÜBECK: CANTATAS: HILF DEINEM VOLK; GOTT, WIE DEIN NAME, Stuttgart Choral Society, Swabian Symphony Orch.; PRELUDES AND FUGUES IN C MINOR AND IN E, Eva Hölderlin, Organ. Vincent Lübeck (1654-1740), contemporary of Bach and Buxtehude, was one of the great figures of the 18th-century North German school. These examples of Lübeck's few surviving works indicate his power and brilliance. Voice and instrument lines in the cantatas are strongly reminiscent of the organ: the preludes and fugues show the influence of Bach and Buxtehude. This is the only recording of the superb cantatas. Text and translation included. "Outstanding record," E. T. Canby, SAT. REVIEW. "Hölderlin's playing is exceptional," AM. RECORD REVIEW. "Will make [Lübeck] many new friends," Philip Miller. (Playing time 37 mins.) HCR 5217 **$2.00**

DONIZETTI: BETLY (LA CAPANNA SVIZZERA), Soloists of Compagnia del Teatro dell'Opera Comica di Roma, Societa del Quartetto, Rome, Chorus and Orch. Betly, a delightful one-act opera written in 1836, is similar in style and story to one of Donizetti's better-known operas, L'Elisir. Betly is lighthearted and farcical, with bright melodies and a freshness characteristic of the best of Donizetti. Libretto (English and Italian) included. "The chief honors go to Angela Tuccari who sings the title role, and the record is worth having for her alone," M. Rayment, GRAMOPHONE REC. REVIEW. "The interpretation . . . is excellent . . . This is a charming record which we recommend to lovers of little-known works," DISQUES.
HCR 5218 **$2.00**

ROSSINI: L'OCCASIONE FA IL LADRO (IL CAMBIO DELLA VALIGIA), Soloists of Compagnia del Teatro dell'Opera Comica di Roma, Societa del Quartetto, Rome, Chorus and Orch. A charming one-act opera buffa, this is one of the first works of Rossini's maturity, and it is filled with the wit, gaiety and sparkle that make his comic operas second only to Mozart's. Like other Rossini works, L'Occasione makes use of the theme of impersonation and attendant amusing confusions. This is the only recording of this important buffa. Full libretto (English and Italian) included. "A major rebirth, a stylish performance . . . the Roman recording engineers have outdone themselves," H. Weinstock, SAT. REVIEW. (Playing time 53 mins.)
HCR 5219 **$2.00**

DOWLAND: "FIRST BOOKE OF AYRES," Pro Musica Antiqua of Brussels, Safford Cape, Director. This is the first recording to include all 22 of the songs of this great collection, written by John Dowland, one of the most important writers of songs of 16th and 17th century England. The participation of the Brussels Pro Musica under Safford Cape insures scholarly accuracy and musical artistry. "Powerfully expressive and very beautiful," B. Haggin. "The musicianly singers . . . never fall below an impressive standard," Philip Miller. Text included. (Playing time 51 mins.) HCR 5220 **$2.00**

FRENCH CHANSONS AND DANCES OF THE 16TH CENTURY, Pro Musica Antiqua of Brussels, Safford Cape, Director. A remarkable selection of 26 three- or four-part chansons and delightful dances from the French Golden Age—by such composers as Orlando Lasso, Crecquillon, Claude Gervaise, etc. Text and translation included. "Delightful, well-varied with respect to mood and to vocal and instrumental color," HIGH FIDELITY. "Performed with . . . discrimination and musical taste, full of melodic distinction and harmonic resource," Irving Kolodin. (Playing time 39 mins.) HCR 5221 **$2.00**

GALUPPI: CONCERTI A QUATRO: #1 IN G MINOR, #2 IN G, #3 IN D, #4 IN C MINOR, #5 IN E FLAT, AND #6 IN B FLAT, Biffoli Quartet. During Baldassare Galuppi's lifetime, his instrumental music was widely renowned, and his contemporaries Mozart and Haydn thought highly of his work. These 6 concerti reflect his great ability; and they are among the most interesting compositions of the period. They are remarkable for their unusual combinations of timbres and for emotional elements that were only then beginning to be introduced into music. Performed by the well-known Biffoli Quartet, this is the only record devoted exclusively to Galuppi. (Playing time 47 mins.) HCR 5222 **$2.00**

HAYDN: DIVERTIMENTI FOR WIND BAND, IN C; IN F; DIVERTIMENTO A NOVE STROMENTI IN C FOR STRINGS AND WIND INSTRUMENTS, reconstructed by H. C. Robbins Landon, performed by members of Vienna State Opera Orch.; MOZART DIVERTIMENTI IN C, III (K. 187) AND IV (K. 188), Salzburg Wind Ensemble. Robbins Landon discovered Haydn manuscripts in a Benedictine monastery in Lower Austria, edited them and restored their original instrumentation The result is this magnificent record. Two little-known divertimenti by Mozart—of great charm and appeal—are also included. None of this music is available elsewhere (Playing time 58 mins.)
HCR 5223 **$2.00**

PURCELL: TRIO SONATAS FROM "SONATAS OF FOUR PARTS" (1697): #9 IN F ("GOLDEN"), #7 IN C, #1 IN B MINOR, #10 IN D, #4 IN D MINOR, #2 IN E FLAT, AND #8 IN G MINOR, Giorgio Ciompi, and Werner Torkanowsky, Violins, Geo. Koutzen, Cello, and Herman Chessid, Harpsichord. These posthumously-published sonatas show Purcell at his most advanced and mature. They are certainly among the finest musical examples of pre-modern chamber music. Those not familiar with his instrumental music are well-advised to hear these outstanding pieces. "Performance sounds excellent," Harold Schonberg. "Some of the most noble and touching music known to anyone," AMERICAN RECORD GUIDE. (Playing time 58 mins.)
HCR 5224 **$2.00**

BARTOK: VIOLIN CONCERTO; SONATA FOR UNACCOMPANIED VIOLIN, Ivry Gitlis, Pro Musica of Vienna, under Hornstein. Both these works are outstanding examples of Bartok's final period, and they show his powers at their fullest. The Violin Concerto is, in the opinion of many authorities, Bartok's finest work, and the Sonata, his last work, is "a masterpiece" (F. Sackville West). "Wonderful, finest performance of both Bartok works I have ever heard," GRAMOPHONE. "Gitlis makes such potent and musical sense out of these works that I suspect many general music lovers (not otherwise in sympathy with modern music) will discover to their amazement that they like it. Exceptionally good sound," AUDITOR. (Playing time 54 mins.)
HCR 5211 **$2.00**

J. S. BACH: PARTITAS FOR UNACCOMPANIED VIOLIN: #2 in D Minor and #3 in E, Bronislav Gimpel. Bach's works for unaccompanied violin fall within the same area that produced the Brandenburg Concerti, the Orchestral Suites, and the first part of the Well-Tempered Clavichord. The D Minor is considered one of Bach's masterpieces; the E Major is a buoyant work with exceptionally interesting bariolage effects. This is the first release of a truly memorable recording by Bronislav Gimpel, "as a violinist, the equal of the greatest" (P. Leron, in OPERA, Paris). (Playing time 53 mins.) HCR 5212 **$2.00**

ROSSINI: QUARTETS FOR WOODWINDS: #1 IN F, #4 IN B FLAT, #5 IN D, AND #6 IN F, N. Y. Woodwind Quartet Members: S. Baron, Flute, J. Barrows, French Horn; B. Garfield, Bassoon; D. Glazer, Clarinet. Rossini's great genius was centered in the opera, but he also wrote a small amount of first-rate non-vocal music. Among these instrumental works, first place is usually given to the very interesting quartets. Of the three different surviving arrangements, this wind group version is the original, and this is the first recording of these works. "Each member of the group displays wonderful virtuosity when the music calls for it, at other times blending sensitively into the ensemble," HIGH FIDELITY. "Sheer delight," Philip Miller. (Playing time 45 mins.) HCR 5214 **$2.00**

TELEMANN: THE GERMAN FANTASIAS FOR HARPSICHORD (#1-12), Helma Elsner. Until recently, Georg Philip Telemann (1681-1767) was one of the mysteriously neglected great men of music. Recently he has received the attention he deserved. He created music that delights modern listeners with its freshness and originality. These fantasias are free in form and reveal the intricacy of thorough bass music, the harmonic wealth of the "new music," and a distinctive melodic beauty. "This is another blessing of the contemporary LP output. Miss Elsner plays with considerable sensitivity and a great deal of understanding," REV. OF RECORDED MUSIC. "Fine recorded sound," Harold Schonberg. "Recommended warmly, very high quality," DISQUES. (Playing time 50 mins.) HCR 5210 **$2.00**

Nova Recordings

In addition to our reprints of outstanding out-of-print records and American releases of first-rate foreign recordings, we have established our own new records. In order to keep every phase of their production under our own control, we have engaged musicians of world renown to play important music (for the most part unavailable elsewhere), have made use of the finest recording studios in New York, and have produced tapes equal to anything on the market, we believe. The first of these entirely new records are now available.

RAVEL: GASPARD DE LA NUIT, LE TOMBEAU DE COUPERIN, JEUX D'EAU, Beveridge Webster, Piano. Webster studied under Ravel and played his works in European recitals, often with Ravel's personal participation in the program. This record offers examples of the three major periods of Ravel's pianistic work, and is a must for any serious collector or music lover. (Playing time about 50 minutes).
Monaural HCR 5213 **$2.00**
Stereo HCR ST 7000 **$2.00**

EIGHTEENTH CENTURY FRENCH FLUTE MUSIC, Jean-Pierre Rampal, Flute, and Robert Veyron-Lacroix, Harpsichord. Contains Concerts Royaux #7 for Flute and Harpsichord in G Minor, Francois Couperin; Sonata dite l'Inconnue in G for Flute and Harpsichord, Michel de la Barre; Sonata #6 in A Minor, Michel Blavet; and Sonata in D Minor, Anne Danican-Philidor. In the opinion of many Rampal is the world's premier flutist. (Playing time about 45 minutes)
Monaural HCR 5238 **$2.00**
Stereo HCR ST 7001 **$2.00**

SCHUMANN: NOVELLETTEN (Opus 21), Beveridge Webster, Piano. Brilliantly played in this original recording by one of America's foremost keyboard performers. Connected Romantic pieces. Long a piano favorite. (Playing time about 45 minutes)
Monaural HCR 5239 **$2.00**
Stereo HCR ST 7002 **$2.00**

Social Sciences

SOCIAL THOUGHT FROM LORE TO SCIENCE, H. E. Barnes and H. Becker. An immense survey of sociological thought and ways of viewing, studying, planning, and reforming society from earliest times to the present. Includes thought on society of preliterate peoples, ancient non-Western cultures, and every great movement in Europe, America, and modern Japan. Analyzes hundreds of great thinkers: Plato, Augustine, Bodin, Vico, Montesquieu, Herder, Comte, Marx, etc. Weighs the contributions of utopians, sophists, fascists and communists; economists, jurists, philosophers, ecclesiastics, and every 19th and 20th century school of scientific sociology, anthropology, and social psychology throughout the world. Combines topical, chronological, and regional approaches, treating the evolution of social thought as a process rather than as a series of mere topics. "Impressive accuracy, competence, and discrimination . . . easily the best single survey," Nation. Thoroughly revised, with new material up to 1960. 2 indexes. Over 2200 bibliographical notes. Three volume set. Total of 1586pp. 5⅜ x 8.
T901 Vol I Paperbound **$2.50**
T902 Vol II Paperbound **$2.50**
T903 Vol III Paperbound **$2.50**
The set **$7.50**

FOLKWAYS, William Graham Sumner. A classic of sociology, a searching and thorough examination of patterns of behaviour from primitive, ancient Greek and Judaic, Medieval Christian, African, Oriental, Melanesian, Australian, Islamic, to modern Western societies. Thousands of illustrations of social, sexual, and religious customs, mores, laws, and institutions. Hundreds of categories: Labor, Wealth, Abortion, Primitive Justice, Life Policy, Slavery, Cannibalism, Uncleanness and the Evil Eye, etc. Will extend the horizon of every reader by showing the relativism of his own culture. Prefatory note by A. G. Keller. Introduction by William Lyon Phelps. Bibliography. Index. xiii + 692pp. 5⅜ x 8. T508 Paperbound **$2.49**

PRIMITIVE RELIGION, P. Radin. A thorough treatment by a noted anthropologist of the nature and origin of man's belief in the supernatural and the influences that have shaped religious expression in primitive societies. Ranging from the Arunta, Ashanti, Aztec, Bushman, Crow, Fijian, etc., of Africa, Australia, Pacific Islands, the Arctic, North and South America, Prof. Radin integrates modern psychology, comparative religion, and economic thought with first-hand accounts gathered by himself and other scholars of primitive initiations, training of the shaman, and other fascinating topics. "Excellent," NATURE (London). Unabridged reissue of 1st edition. New author's preface. Bibliographic notes. Index. x + 322pp. 5⅜ x 8.
T393 Paperbound **$2.00**

PRIMITIVE MAN AS PHILOSOPHER, P. Radin. A standard anthropological work covering primitive thought on such topics as the purpose of life, marital relations, freedom of thought, symbolism, death, resignation, the nature of reality, personality, gods, and many others. Drawn from factual material gathered from the Winnebago, Oglala Sioux, Maori, Baganda, Batak, Zuni, among others, it does not distort ideas by removing them from context but interprets strictly within the original framework. Extensive selections of original primitive documents. Bibliography. Index. xviii + 402pp. 5⅜ x 8. T392 Paperbound **$2.25**

A TREATISE ON SOCIOLOGY, THE MIND AND SOCIETY, Vilfredo Pareto. This treatise on human society is one of the great classics of modern sociology. First published in 1916, its careful catalogue of the innumerable manifestations of non-logical human conduct (Book One); the theory of "residues," leading to the premise that sentiment not logic determines human behavior (Book Two), and of "derivations," beliefs derived from desires (Book Three); and the general description of society made up of non-elite and elite, consisting of "foxes" who live by cunning and "lions" who live by force, stirred great controversy. But Pareto's passion for isolation and classification of elements and factors, and his allegiance to scientific method as the key tool for scrutinizing the human situation made his a truly twentieth-century mind and his work a catalytic influence on certain later social commentators. These four volumes (bound as two) require no special training to be appreciated and any reader who wishes to gain a complete understanding of modern sociological theory, regardless of special field of interest, will find them a must. Reprint of revised (corrected) printing of original edition. Translated by Andrew Bongiorno and Arthur Livingston. Index. Bibliography. Appendix containing index-summary of theorems. 48 diagrams. Four volumes bound as two. Total of 2063pp. 5⅜ x 8½. The set Clothbound **$15.00**

THE POLISH PEASANT IN EUROPE AND AMERICA, William I. Thomas, Florian Znaniecki. A seminal sociological study of peasant primary groups (family and community) and the disruptions produced by a new industrial system and immigration to America. The peasant's family, class system, religious and aesthetic attitudes, and economic life are minutely examined and analyzed in hundreds of pages of primary documentation, particularly letters between family members. The disorientation caused by new environments is scrutinized in detail (a 312-page autobiography of an immigrant is especially valuable and revealing) in an attempt to find common experiences and reactions. The famous "Methodological Note" sets forth the principles which guided the authors. When out of print this set has sold for as much as $50. 2nd revised edition. 2 vols. Vol. 1: xv + 1115pp. Vol. 2: 1135pp. Index. 6 x 9.
T478 Clothbound 2 vol. set **$12.50**

Art, History of Art, Antiques, Graphic Arts, Handcrafts

ART STUDENTS' ANATOMY, E. J. Farris. Outstanding art anatomy that uses chiefly living objects for its illustrations. 71 photos of undraped men, women, children are accompanied by carefully labeled matching sketches to illustrate the skeletal system, articulations and movements, bony landmarks, the muscular system, skin, fasciae, fat, etc. 9 x-ray photos show movement of joints. Undraped models are shown in such actions as serving in tennis, drawing a bow in archery, playing football, dancing, preparing to spring and to dive. Also discussed and illustrated are proportions, age and sex differences, the anatomy of the smile, etc. 8 plates by the great early 18th century anatomic illustrator Siegfried Albinus are also included. Glossary. 158 figures, 7 in color. x + 159pp. 5⅝ x 8⅜. T744 Paperbound **$1.50**

AN ATLAS OF ANATOMY FOR ARTISTS, F Schider. A new 3rd edition of this standard text enlarged by 52 new illustrations of hands, anatomical studies by Cloquet, and expressive life studies of the body by Barcsay. 189 clear, detailed plates offer you precise information of impeccable accuracy. 29 plates show all aspects of the skeleton, with closeups of special areas, while 54 full-page plates, mostly in two colors, give human musculature as seen from four different points of view, with cutaways for important portions of the body. 14 full-page plates provide photographs of hand forms, eyelids, female breasts, and indicate the location of muscles upon models. 59 additional plates show how great artists of the past utilized human anatomy. They reproduce sketches and finished work by such artists as Michelangelo, Leonardo da Vinci, Goya, and 15 others. This is a lifetime reference work which will be one of the most important books in any artist's library. "The standard reference tool," AMERICAN LIBRARY ASSOCIATION. "Excellent," AMERICAN ARTIST. Third enlarged edition. 189 plates, 647 illustrations. xxvi + 192pp. 7⅞ x 10⅝. T241 Clothbound **$6.00**

AN ATLAS OF ANIMAL ANATOMY FOR ARTISTS, W. Ellenberger, H. Baum, H. Dittrich. The largest, richest animal anatomy for artists available in English. 99 detailed anatomical plates of such animals as the horse, dog, cat, lion, deer, seal, kangaroo, flying squirrel, cow, bull, goat, monkey, hare, and bat. Surface features are clearly indicated, while progressive beneath-the-skin pictures show musculature, tendons, and bone structure. Rest and action are exhibited in terms of musculature and skeletal structure and detailed cross-sections are given for heads and important features. The animals chosen are representative of specific families so that a study of these anatomies will provide knowledge of hundreds of related species. "Highly recommended as one of the very few books on the subject worthy of being used as an authoritative guide," DESIGN. "Gives a fundamental knowledge," AMERICAN ARTIST. Second revised, enlarged edition with new plates from Cuvier, Stubbs, etc. 288 illustrations. 153pp. 11⅜ x 9. T82 Clothbound **$6.00**

THE HUMAN FIGURE IN MOTION, Eadweard Muybridge. The largest selection in print of Muybridge's famous high-speed action photos of the human figure in motion. 4789 photographs illustrate 162 different actions: men, women, children—mostly undraped—are shown walking, running, carrying various objects, sitting, lying down, climbing, throwing, arising, and performing over 150 other actions. Some actions are shown in as many as 150 photographs each. All in all there are more than 500 action strips in this enormous volume, series shots taken at shutter speeds of as high as 1/6000th of a second! These are not posed shots, but true stopped motion. They show bone and muscle in situations that the human eye is not fast enough to capture. Earlier, smaller editions of these prints have brought $40 and more on the out-of-print market. "A must for artists," ART IN FOCUS. "An unparalleled dictionary of action for all artists," AMERICAN ARTIST. 390 full-page plates, with 4789 photographs. Printed on heavy glossy stock. Reinforced binding with headbands. xxi + 390pp. 7⅞ x 10⅝. T204 Clothbound **$10.00**

ANIMALS IN MOTION, Eadweard Muybridge. This is the largest collection of animal action photos in print. 34 different animals (horses, mules, oxen, goats, camels, pigs, cats, guanacos, lions, gnus, deer, monkeys, eagles—and 21 others) in 132 characteristic actions. The horse alone is shown in more than 40 different actions. All 3919 photographs are taken in series at speeds up to 1/6000th of a second. The secrets of leg motion, spinal patterns, head movements, strains and contortions shown nowhere else are captured. You will see exactly how a lion sets his foot down; how an elephant's knees are like a human's—and how they differ; the position of a kangaroo's legs in mid-leap; how an ostrich's head bobs; details of the flight of birds—and thousands of facets of motion only the fastest cameras can catch. Photographed from domestic animals and animals in the Philadelphia zoo, it contains neither semiposed artificial shots nor distorted telephoto shots taken under adverse conditions. Artists, biologists, decorators, cartoonists, will find this book indispensable for understanding animals in motion. "A really marvelous series of plates," NATURE (London). "The dry plate's most spectacular early use was by Eadweard Muybridge," LIFE. 3919 photographs; 380 full pages of plates. 440pp. Printed on heavy glossy paper. Deluxe binding with headbands. 7⅞ x 10⅝. T203 Clothbound **$10.00**

ART ANATOMY, William Rimmer, M.D. Often called one of America's foremost contributions to art instruction, a work of art in its own right. More than 700 line drawings by the author, first-rate anatomist and dissector as well as artist, with a non-technical anatomical text. Impeccably accurate drawings of muscles, skeletal structure, surface features, other aspects of males and females, children, adults and aged persons show not only form, size, insertion and articulation but personality and emotion as reflected by physical features usually ignored in modern anatomical works. Complete unabridged reproduction of 1876 edition slightly rearranged. Introduction by Robert Hutchinson. 722 illustrations. xiii + 153pp. 7¾ x 10¾.
T908 Paperbound **$2.00**

ANIMAL DRAWING: ANATOMY AND ACTION FOR ARTISTS, C. R. Knight. The author and illustrator of this work was "the most distinguished painter of animal life." This extensive course in animal drawing discusses musculature, bone structure, animal psychology, movements, habits, habitats. Innumerable tips on proportions, light and shadow play, coloring, hair formation, feather arrangement, scales, how animals lie down, animal expressions, etc., from great apes to birds. Pointers on avoiding gracelessness in horses, deer; on introducing proper power and bulk to heavier animals; on giving proper grace and subtle expression to members of the cat family. Originally titled "Animal Anatomy and Psychology for the Artist and Layman." Over 123 illustrations. 149pp. 8¼ x 10½. T426 Paperbound **$2.00**

DESIGN FOR ARTISTS AND CRAFTSMEN, L. Wolchonok. The most thorough course ever prepared on the creation of art motifs and designs. It teaches you to create your own designs out of things around you — from geometric patterns, plants, birds, animals, humans, landscapes, and man-made objects. It leads you step by step through the creation of more than 1300 designs, and shows you how to create design that is fresh, well-founded, and original. Mr. Wolchonok, whose text is used by scores of art schools, shows you how the same idea can be developed into many different forms, ranging from near representationalism to the most advanced forms of abstraction. The material in this book is entirely new, and combines full awareness of traditional design with the work of such men as Miro, Léger, Picasso, Moore, and others. 113 detailed exercises, with instruction hints, diagrams, and details to enable you to apply Wolchonok's methods to your own work. "A great contribution to the field of design and crafts," N. Y. SOCIETY OF CRAFTSMEN. More than 1300 illustrations. xv + 207pp. 7⅞ x 10¾. T274 Clothbound **$4.95**

HAWTHORNE ON PAINTING. A vivid recreation, from students' notes, of instruction by Charles W. Hawthorne, given for over 31 years at his famous Cape Cod School of Art. Divided into sections on the outdoor model, still life, landscape, the indoor model, and water color, each section begins with a concise essay, followed by epigrammatic comments on color, form, seeing, etc. Not a formal course, but comments of a great teacher-painter on specific student works, which will solve problems in your own painting and understanding of art. "An excellent introduction for laymen and students alike," Time. Introduction. 100pp. 5⅜ x 8.
T653 Paperbound **$1.00**

THE ENJOYMENT AND USE OF COLOR, Walter Sargent. This book explains fascinating relations among colors, between colors in nature and art; describes experiments that you can perform to understand these relations more thoroughly; points out hundreds of little known facts about color values, intensities, effects of high and low illumination, complementary colors, color harmonies. Practical hints for painters, references to techniques of masters, questions at chapter ends for self-testing all make this a valuable book for artists, professional and amateur, and for general readers interested in world of color. Republication of 1923 edition. 35 illustrations, 6 full-page plates. New color frontispiece. Index. xii + 274pp. 5⅜ x 8. T944 Paperbound **$2.25**

DECORATIVE ALPHABETS AND INITIALS, ed. by Alexander Nesbitt. No payment, no permission needed to reproduce any one of these 3924 different letters, covering 1000 years. Crisp, clear letters all in line, from Anglo-Saxon mss., Luebeck Cathedral, 15th century Augsburg; the work of Dürer, Holbein, Cresci, Beardsley, Rossing Wadsworth, John Moylin, etc. Every imaginable style. 91 complete alphabets. 123 full-page plates. 192pp. 7¾ x 10¾.
T544 Paperbound **$2.25**

THREE CLASSICS OF ITALIAN CALLIGRAPHY, edited by Oscar Ogg. Here, combined in a single volume, are complete reproductions of three famous calligraphic works written by the greatest writing masters of the Renaissance: Arrighi's OPERINA and IL MODO, Tagliente's LO PRESENTE LIBRO, and Palatino's LIBRO NUOVO. These books present more than 200 complete alphabets and thousands of lettered specimens. The basic hand is Papal Chancery, but scores of other alphabets are also given: European and Asiatic local alphabets, foliated and art alphabets, scrolls, cartouches, borders, etc. Text is in Italian. Introduction. 245 plates. x + 272pp. 6⅛ x 9¼. T212 Paperbound **$2.25**

CALLIGRAPHY, J. G. Schwandner. One of the legendary books in the graphic arts, copies of which brought $500 each on the rare book market, now reprinted for the first time in over 200 years. A beautiful plate book of graceful calligraphy, and an inexhaustible source of first-rate material copyright-free, for artists, and directors, craftsmen, commercial artists, etc. More than 300 ornamental initials forming 12 complete alphabets, over 150 ornate frames and panels, over 200 flourishes, over 75 calligraphic pictures including a temple, cherubs, cocks, dodos, stags, chamois, foliated lions, greyhounds, etc. Thousand of calligraphic elements to be used for suggestions of quality, sophistication, antiquity, and sheer beauty. Historical introduction. 158 full-page plates. 368pp. 9 x 13.
T475 Clothbound **$10.00**

THE HISTORY AND TECHNIQUE OF LETTERING, A. Nesbitt. The only thorough inexpensive history of letter forms from the point of view of the artist. Mr. Nesbitt covers every major development in lettering from the ancient Egyptians to the present and illustrates each development with a complete alphabet. Such masters as Baskerville, Bell, Bodoni, Caslon, Koch, Kilian, Morris, Garamont, Jenson, and dozens of others are analyzed in terms of artistry and historical development. The author also presents a 65-page practical course in lettering, besides the full historical text. 89 complete alphabets; 165 additional lettered specimens. xvii + 300pp. 5⅜ x 8. T427 Paperbound **$2.00**

FOOT-HIGH LETTERS: A GUIDE TO LETTERING (A PRACTICAL SYLLABUS FOR TEACHERS), M. Price. A complete alphabet of Classic Roman letters, each a foot high, each on a separate 16 x 22 plate—perfect for use in lettering classes. In addition to an accompanying description, each plate also contains 9 two-inch-high forms of letter in various type faces, such as "Caslon," "Empire," "Onyx," and "Neuland," illustrating the many possible derivations from the standard classical forms. One plate contains 21 additional forms of the letter A. The fully illustrated 16-page syllabus by Mr. Price, formerly of the Pratt Institute and the Rhode Island School of Design, contains dozens of useful suggestions for student and teacher alike. An indispensable teaching aid. Extensively revised. 16-page syllabus and 30 plates in slip cover, 16 x 22. T239 Clothbound **$6.00**

THE STYLES OF ORNAMENT, Alexander Speltz. Largest collection of ornaments in print—3765 illustrations of prehistoric, Lombard, Gothic, Frank, Romanesque, Mohammedan, Renaissance, Polish, Swiss, Rococo, Sheraton, Empire, U. S. Colonial, etc., ornament. Gargoyles, dragons, columns, necklaces, urns, friezes, furniture, buildings, keyholes, tapestries, fantastic animals, armor, religious objects, much more, all in line. Reproduce any one free. Index. Bibliography. 400 plates. 656pp. 5⅝ x 8⅜. T557 Paperbound **$2.50**

HANDBOOK OF DESIGNS AND DEVICES, C. P. Hornung. This unique book is indispensable to the designer, commercial artist, and hobbyist. It is not a textbook but a working collection of 1836 basic designs and variations, carefully reproduced, which may be used without permission. Variations of circle, line, band, triangle, square, cross, diamond, swastika, pentagon, octagon, hexagon, star, scroll, interlacement, shields, etc. Supplementary notes on the background and symbolism of the figures. "A necessity to every designer who would be original without having to labor heavily," ARTIST AND ADVERTISER. 204 plates. 240pp. 5⅜ x 8. T125 Paperbound **$2.00**

THE UNIVERSAL PENMAN, George Bickham. This beautiful book, which first appeared in 1743, is the largest collection of calligraphic specimens, flourishes, alphabets, and calligraphic illustrations ever published. 212 full-page plates are drawn from the work of such 18th century masters of English roundhand as Dove, Champion, Bland, and 20 others. They contain 22 complete alphabets, over 2,000 flourishes, and 122 illustrations, each drawn with a stylistic grace impossible to describe. This book is invaluable to anyone interested in the beauties of calligraphy, or to any artist, hobbyist, or craftsman who wishes to use the very best ornamental handwriting and flourishes for decorative purposes. Commercial artists, advertising artists, have found it unexcelled as a source of material suggesting quality. "An essential part of any art library, and a book of permanent value," AMERICAN ARTIST. 212 plates. 224pp. 9 x 13¾. T20 Clothbound **$10.00**

1800 WOODCUTS BY THOMAS BEWICK AND HIS SCHOOL. Prepared by Dover's editorial staff, this is the largest collection of woodcuts by Bewick and his school ever compiled. Contains the complete engravings from all his major works and a wide range of illustrations from lesser-known collections, all photographed from clear copies of the original books and reproduced in line. Carefully and conveniently organized into sections on Nature (animals and birds, scenery and landscapes, plants, insects, etc.), People (love and courtship, social life, school and domestic scenes, misfortunes, costumes, etc.), Business and Trade, and illustrations from primers, fairytales, spelling books, frontispieces, borders, fables and allegories, etc. In addition to technical proficiency and simple beauty, Bewick's work is remarkable as a mode of pictorial symbolism, reflecting rustic tranquility, an atmosphere of rest, simplicity, idyllic contentment. A delight for the eye, an inexhaustible source of illustrative material for art studios, commercial artists, advertising agencies. Individual illustrations (up to 10 for any one use) are copyright free. Classified index. Bibliography and sources. Introduction by Robert Hutchinson. 1800 woodcuts. xiv + 247pp. 9 x 12. T766 Clothbound **$10.00**

A HANDBOOK OF EARLY ADVERTISING ART, C. P. Hornung. The largest collection of copyright-free early advertising art ever compiled. Vol. I contains some 2,000 illustrations of agricultural devices, animals, old automobiles, birds, buildings, Christmas decorations (with 7 Santa Clauses by Nast), allegorical figures, fire engines, horses and vehicles, Indians, portraits, sailing ships, trains, sports, trade cuts — and 30 other categories! Vol. II, devoted to typography, has over 4000 specimens: 600 different Roman, Gothic, Barnum, Old English faces; 630 ornamental type faces; 1115 initials, hundreds of scrolls, flourishes, etc. This third edition is enlarged by 78 additional plates containing all new material. "A remarkable collection," PRINTERS' INK. "A rich contribution to the history of American design," GRAPHIS.
Volume I, Pictorial. Over 2000 illustrations. xiv + 242pp. 9 x 12. T122 Clothbound **$10.00**
Volume II, Typographical. Over 4000 specimens. vii + 312pp. 9 x 12. T123 Clothbound **$10.00**
Two volume set, T121 Clothbound, only **$18.50**

New Books

101 PATCHWORK PATTERNS, Ruby Short McKim. With no more ability than the fundamentals of ordinary sewing, you will learn to make over 100 beautiful quilts: flowers, rainbows, Irish chains, fish and bird designs, leaf designs, unusual geometric patterns, many others. Cutting designs carefully diagrammed and described, suggestions for materials, yardage estimates, step-by-step instructions, plus entertaining stories of origins of quilt names, other folklore. Revised 1962. 101 full-sized patterns. 140 illustrations. Index. 128pp. 7⅞ x 10¾.
T773 Paperbound **$1.85**

ESSENTIAL GRAMMAR SERIES
By concentrating on the essential core of material that constitutes the semantically most important forms and areas of a language and by stressing explanation (often bringing parallel English forms into the discussion) rather than rote memory, this new series of grammar books is among the handiest language aids ever devised. Designed by linguists and teachers for adults with limited learning objectives and learning time, these books omit nothing important, yet they teach more usable language material and do it more quickly and permanently than any other self-study material. Clear and rigidly economical, they concentrate upon immediately usable language material, logically organized so that related material is always presented together. Any reader of typical capability can use them to refresh his grasp of language, to supplement self-study language records or conventional grammars used in schools, or to begin language study on his own. Now available:

ESSENTIAL GERMAN GRAMMAR, Dr. Guy Stern & E. F. Bleiler. Index. Glossary of terms. 128pp. 5⅜ x 8.
T422 Paperbound **$1.00**

ESSENTIAL FRENCH GRAMMAR, Dr. Seymour Resnick. Index. Cognate list. Glossary. 159pp. 5⅜ x 8.
T419 Paperbound **$1.00**

ESSENTIAL ITALIAN GRAMMAR, Dr. Olga Ragusa. Index. Glossary. 111pp. 5⅜ x 8.
T779 Paperbound **$1.00**

ESSENTIAL SPANISH GRAMMAR, Dr. Seymour Resnick. Index. 50-page cognate list. Glossary. 138pp. 5⅜ x 8.
T780 Paperbound **$1.00**

PHILOSOPHIES OF MUSIC HISTORY: A Study of General Histories of Music, 1600-1960, Warren D. Allen. Unquestionably one of the most significant documents yet to appear in musicology, this thorough survey covers the entire field of historical research in music. An influential masterpiece of scholarship, it includes early music histories; theories on the ethos of music; lexicons, dictionaries and encyclopedias of music; musical historiography through the centuries; philosophies of music history; scores of related topics. Copiously documented. New preface brings work up to 1960. Index. 317-item bibliography. 9 illustrations; 3 full-page plates. 5⅜ x 8½. xxxiv + 382pp.
T282 Paperbound **$2.00**

MR. DOOLEY ON IVRYTHING AND IVRYBODY, Finley Peter Dunne. The largest collection in print of hilarious utterances by the irrepressible Irishman of Archey Street, one of the most vital characters in American fiction. Gathered from the half dozen books that appeared during the height of Mr. Dooley's popularity, these 102 pieces are all unaltered and uncut, and they are all remarkably fresh and pertinent even today. Selected and edited by Robert Hutchinson. 5⅜ x 8½. xii + 244p.
T626 Paperbound **$1.00**

TREATISE ON PHYSIOLOGICAL OPTICS, Hermann von Helmholtz. Despite new investigations, this important work will probably remain preeminent. Contains everything known about physiological optics up to 1925, covering scores of topics under the general headings of dioptrics of the eye, sensations of vision, and perecptions of vision. Von Helmholtz's voluminous data are all included, as are extensive supplementary matter incorporated into the third German edition, new material prepared for 1925 English edition, and copious textual annotations by J. P. C. Southall. The most exhaustive treatise ever prepared on the subject, it has behind it a list of contributors that will never again be duplicated. Translated and edited by J. P. C. Southall. Bibliography. Indexes. 312 illustrations. 3 volumes bound as 2. Total of 1749pp. 5⅜ x 8.
S15-16 Two volume set, Clothbound **$15.00**

THE ARTISTIC ANATOMY OF TREES, Rex Vicat Cole. Even the novice with but an elementary knowledge of drawing and none of the structure of trees can learn to draw, paint trees from this systematic, lucid instruction book. Copiously illustrated with the author's own sketches, diagrams, and 50 paintings from the early Renaissance to today, it covers composition; structure of twigs, boughs, buds, branch systems; outline forms of major species; how leaf is set on twig; flowers and fruit and their arrangement; etc. 500 illustrations. Bibliography. Indexes. 347pp. 5⅜ x 8.
T1016 Clothbound **$4.50**

HOW PLANTS GET THEIR NAMES, L. H. Bailey. In this basic introduction to botanical nomenclature, a famed expert on plants and plant life reveals the confusion that can result from misleading common names of plants and points out the fun and advantage of using a sound, scientific approach. Covers every aspect of the subject, including an historical survey beginning before Linnaeus systematized nomenclature, the literal meaning of scores of Latin names, their English equivalents, etc. Enthusiastically written and easy to follow, this handbook for gardeners, amateur horticulturalists, and beginning botany students is knowledgeable, accurate and useful. 11 illustrations. Lists of Latin, English botanical names. 192pp. 5⅜ x 8½. T796 Paperbound **$1.15**

PIERRE CURIE, Marie Curie. Nobel Prize winner creates a memorable portrait of her equally famous husband in a fine scientific biography. Recounting his childhood, his haphazard education, and his experimental research (with his brother) in the physics of crystals, Mme. Curie brings to life the strong, determined personality of a great scientist at work and discusses, in clear, straightforward terms, her husband's and her own work with radium and radioactivity. A great book about two very great founders of modern science. Includes Mme. Curie's autobiographical notes. Translated by Charlotte and Vernon Kellogg. viii + 120pp. 5⅜ x 8½. T199 Paperbound **$1.00**

STYLES IN PAINTING: A Comparative Study, Paul Zucker. Professor of Art History at Cooper Union presents an important work of art-understanding that will guide you to a fuller, deeper appreciation of masterpieces of art and at the same time add to your understanding of how they fit into the evolution of style from the earliest times to this century. Discusses general principles of historical method and aesthetics, history of styles, then illustrates with more than 230 great paintings organized by subject matter so you can see at a glance how styles have changed through the centuries. 236 beautiful halftones. xiv + 338pp. 5⅝ x 8½. T760 Paperbound **$2.00**

NEW VARIORUM EDITION OF SHAKESPEARE

One of the monumental feats of Shakespeare scholarship is the famous New Variorum edition, containing full texts of the plays together with an entire reference library worth of historical and critical information: all the variant readings that appear in the quartos and folios; annotations by leading scholars from the earliest days of Shakespeare criticism to the date of publication; essays on meaning, background, productions by Johnson, Addison, Fielding, Lessing, Hazlitt, Coleridge, Ulrici, Swinburne, and other major Shakespeare critics; original sources of Shakespeare's inspiration. For the first time, this definitive edition of Shakespeare's plays, each printed in a separate volume, will be available in inexpensive editions to scholars, to teachers and students, and to every lover of Shakespeare and fine literature. Now ready:

KING LEAR, edited by Horace Howard Furness. Bibliography. List of editions collated in notes. viii + 503pp. 5⅜ x 8½. T1000 Paperbound **$2.25**

MACBETH, edited by Horace Howard Furness Jr. Bibliography. List of editions collated in notes. xvi + 562pp. 5⅜ x 8½. T1001 Paperbound **$2.25**

ROMEO AND JULIET, edited by Horace Howard Furness. Bibliography. List of editions collated in notes. xxvi + 480pp. 5⅜ x 8½. T1002 Paperbound **$2.25**

OTTHELLO, edited by Horace Howard Furness. Bibliography. List of editions collated in notes. x + 471pp. 5⅜ x 8½. T1003 Paperbound **$2.25**

HAMLET, edited by Horace Howard Furness. Bibliography. List of editions collated in notes. Total of 926pp. 5⅜ x 8½. T1004-1005 Two volume set, Paperbound **$4.50**

THE GARDENER'S YEAR, Karel Capek. The author of this refreshingly funny book is probably best known in U. S. as the author of "R. U. R.," a biting satire on the machine age. Here, his satiric genius finds expression in a wholly different vein: a warm, witty chronicle of the joys and trials of the amateur gardener as he watches over his plants, his soil and the weather from January to December. 59 drawings by Joseph Capek add an important second dimension to the fun. "Mr. Capek writes with sympathy, understanding and humor," NEW YORK TIMES. "Will delight the amateur gardener, and indeed everyone else," SATURDAY REVIEW. Translated by M. and R. Weatherall. 59 illustrations. 159pp. 4½ x 6½. T1014 Paperbound **$1.00**

THE ADVANCE OF THE FUNGI, E. C. Large. The dramatic story of the battle against fungi, from the year the potato blight hit Europe (1845) to 1940, and of men who fought and won it: Pasteur, Anton de Bary, Tulasne, Berkeley, Woronin, Jensen, many others. Combines remarkable grasp of facts and their significance with skill to write dramatic, exciting prose. "Philosophically witty, fundamentally thoughtful, always mature," NEW YORK HERALD TRIBUNE. "Highly entertaining, intelligent, penetrating," NEW YORKER. Bibliography. 64 illustrations. 6 full-page plates. 488pp. 5⅜ x 8½. T437 Paperbound **$2.25**

THE PAINTER'S METHODS AND MATERIALS, A. P. Laurie. Adviser to the British Royal Academy discusses the ills that paint is heir to and the methods most likely to counteract them. Examining 48 masterpieces by Fra Lippo Lippi, Millais, Boucher, Rembrandt, Romney, Van Eyck, Velazquez, Michaelangelo, Botticelli, Frans Hals, Turner, and others, he tries to discover how special and unique effects were achieved. Not conjectural information, but certain and authoritative. Beautiful, sharp reproductions, plus textual illustrations of apparatus and the results of experiments with pigments and media. 63 illustrations and diagrams. Index. 250pp. 5⅜ x 8. T1019 Clothbound **$3.75**

CHANCE, LUCK AND STATISTICS, H. C. Levinson. The theory of chance, or probability, and the science of statistics presented in simple, non-technical language. Covers fundamentals by analyzing games of chance, then applies those fundamentals to immigration and birth rates, operations research, stock speculation, insurance rates, advertising, and other fields. Excellent course supplement and a delightful introduction for non-mathematicians. Formerly "The Science of Chance." Index. xiv + 356pp. 5⅜ x 8. T1007 Paperbound **$1.85**

THROUGH THE ALIMENTARY CANAL WITH GUN AND CAMERA: A Fascinating Trip to the Interior, George S. Chappell. An intrepid explorer, better known as a major American humorist, accompanied by imaginary camera-man and botanist, conducts this unforgettably hilarious journey to the human interior. Wildly imaginative, his account satirizes academic pomposity, parodies cliché-ridden travel literature, and cleverly uses facts of physiology for comic purposes. All the original line drawings by Otto Soglow are included to add to the merriment. Preface by Robert Benchley. 17 illustrations. xii + 116pp. 5⅜ x 8½. T376 Paperbound **$1.00**

TALKS TO TEACHERS ON PSYCHOLOGY and to Students on Some of Life's Ideals, William James. America's greatest psychologist invests these lectures with immense personal charm, invaluable insights, and superb literary style. 15 Harvard lectures, 3 lectures delivered to students in New England touch upon psychology and the teaching of art, stream of consciousness, the child as a behaving organism, education and behavior, association of ideas, the gospel of relaxation, what makes life significant, and other related topics. Interesting, and still vital pedagogy. x + 146pp. 5⅜ x 8½. T261 Paperbound **$1.00**

A WHIMSEY ANTHOLOGY, collected by Carolyn Wells. Delightful verse on the lighter side: logical whimsies, poems shaped like decanters and flagons, lipograms and acrostics, alliterative verse, enigmas and charades, anagrams, linguistic and dialectic verse, tongue twisters, limericks, travesties, and just about very other kind of whimsical poetry ever written. Works by Edward Lear, Gelett Burgess, Poe, Lewis Carroll, Henley, Robert Herrick, Christina Rossetti, scores of other poets will entertain and amuse you for hours. Index. xiv + 221pp. 5⅜ x 8½. T1020 Paperbound **$1.25**

LANDSCAPE PAINTING, R. O. Dunlop. A distinguished modern artist is a perfect guide to the aspiring landscape painter. This practical book imparts to even the uninitiated valuable methods and techniques. Useful advice is interwoven throughout a fascinating illustrated history of landscape painting, from Ma Yüan to Picasso. 60 half-tone reproductions of works by Giotto, Giovanni Bellini, Piero della Francesca, Tintoretto, Giorgione, Raphael, Van Ruisdael, Poussin, Gainsborough, Monet, Cezanne, Seurat, Picasso, many others. Total of 71 illustrations, 4 in color. Index. 192pp. 7⅜ x 10. T1018 Clothbound **$6.00**

PRACTICAL LANDSCAPE PAINTING, Adrian Stokes. A complete course in landscape painting that trains the senses to perceive as well as the hand to apply the principles underlying the pictorial aspect of nature. Author fully explains tools, value and nature of various colors, and instructs beginners in clear, simple terms how to apply them. Places strong emphasis on drawing and composition, foundations often neglected in painting texts. Includes pictorial-textual survey of the art from Ancient China to the present, with helpful critical comments and numerous diagrams illustrating every stage. 93 illustrations. Index. 256pp. 5⅜ x 8. T1017 Clothbound **$3.75**

PELLUCIDAR, THREE NOVELS: AT THE EARTH'S CORE, PELLUCIDAR, TANAR OF PELLUCIDAR, Edgar Rice Burroughs. The first three novels of adventure in the thrill-filled world within the hollow interior of the earth. David Innes's mechanical mole drills through the outer crust and precipitates him into an astonishing world. Among Burroughs's most popular work. Illustrations by J. Allan St. John. 5⅜ x 8½. T1051 Paperbound **$2.00**
T1050 Clothbound **$3.75**

JOE MILLER'S JESTS OR, THE WITS VADE-MECUM. Facsimile of the first edition of famous 18th century collection of repartees, bons mots, puns and jokes, the father of the humor anthology. A first-hand look at the taste of fashionable London in the Age of Pope. 247 entertaining anecdotes, many involving well-known personages such as Colley Cibber, Sir Thomas More, Rabelais, rich in humor, historic interest. New introduction contains biographical information on Joe Miller, fascinating history of his enduring collection, bibliographical information on collections of comic material. Introduction by Robert Hutchinson. 96pp. 5⅜ x 8½. Paperbound **$1.00**

THE HUMOROUS WORLD OF JEROME K. JEROME. Complete essays and extensive passages from nine out-of-print books ("Three Men on Wheels," "Novel Notes," "Told After Supper," "Sketches in Lavender, Blue and Green," "American Wives and Others," 4 more) by a highly original humorist, author of the novel "Three Men in a Boat." Human nature is JKJ's subject: the problems of husbands, of wives, of tourists, of the human animal trapped in the drawing room. His sympathetic acceptance of the shortcomings of his race and his ability to see humor in almost any situation make this a treasure for those who know his work and a pleasant surprise for those who don't. Edited and with an introduction by Robert Hutchinson. xii + 260pp. 5⅜ x 8½. T58 Paperbound **$1.00**